PRENTICE HALL

SCIENCE EXPLORER

Earth's Changing Surface

Prentice
Hall

Needham, Massachusetts
Upper Saddle River, New Jersey
Glenview, Illinois

Earth's Changing Surface

Book-Specific Resources

Student Edition
Annotated Teacher's Edition
Teaching Resources with Color Transparencies
Consumable and Nonconsumable Materials Kits
Guided Reading Audio CDs
Guided Reading Audiotapes
Guided Reading and Study Workbook
Guided Reading and Study Workbook, Teacher's Edition
Lab Activity Videotapes
Science Explorer Videotapes
Science Explorer Web Site at **www.phschool.com**

Program-Wide Resources

Computer Test Bank Book with CD-ROM
How to Assess Student Work
How to Manage Instruction in the Block
Inquiry Skills Activity Book
Integrated Science Laboratory Manual
Integrated Science Laboratory Manual, Teacher's Edition
Interactive Student Tutorial CD-ROM
Prentice Hall Interdisciplinary Explorations
Probeware Lab Manual
Product Testing Activities by Consumer Reports™
Program Planning Guide
Reading in the Content Area with Literature Connections
Resource Pro® CD-ROM (Teaching Resources on CD-ROM)
Science Explorer Videodiscs
Standardized Test Preparation Book
Student-Centered Science Activity Books
Teacher's ELL Handbook: Strategies for English Language Learners

Spanish Resources

Spanish Student Edition
Spanish Guided Reading Audio CDs with Section Summaries
Spanish Guided Reading Audiotapes with Section Summaries
Spanish Science Explorer Videotapes

Science Explorer Student Editions

From Bacteria to Plants

Animals

Cells and Heredity

Human Biology and Health

Environmental Science

Inside Earth

Earth's Changing Surface

Earth's Waters

Weather and Climate

Astronomy

Chemical Building Blocks

Chemical Interactions

Motion, Forces, and Energy

Electricity and Magnetism

Sound and Light

Cover: One of the many red sandstone arches in Arches National Park, Utah

Acknowledgments

Excerpt from *Dust Storm Disaster* on page 59 by Woody Guthrie. Copyright © 1960 (Renewed) by Ludlow Music, Inc. c/o The Richmond Organization. All rights reserved. Used by permission.

Excerpt from *The Hymn to Hapy* on page 145 by Miriam Lichtheim. Copyright ©1973-1980 Regents of the University of California.

ISBN 0-13-054078-1

5 6 7 8 9 10   05 04 03

Program Authors

Michael J. Padilla, Ph.D.
Professor
Department of Science Education
University of Georgia
Athens, Georgia

Michael Padilla is a leader in middle school science education. He has served as an editor and elected officer for the National Science Teachers Association. He has been principal investigator of several National Science Foundation and Eisenhower grants and served as a writer of the National Science Education Standards.

As lead author of *Science Explorer,* Mike has inspired the team in developing a program that meets the needs of middle grades students, promotes science inquiry, and is aligned with the National Science Education Standards.

Ioannis Miaoulis, Ph.D.
Dean of Engineering
College of Engineering
Tufts University
Medford, Massachusetts

Martha Cyr, Ph.D.
Director, Engineering
   Educational Outreach
College of Engineering
Tufts University
Medford, Massachusetts

Science Explorer was created in collaboration with the College of Engineering at Tufts University. Tufts has an extensive engineering outreach program that uses engineering design and construction to excite and motivate students and teachers in science and technology education.

Faculty from Tufts University participated in the development of *Science Explorer* chapter projects, reviewed the student books for content accuracy, and helped coordinate field testing.

Book Author

Joseph D. Exline, Ed.D.
Former Director of Science
Virginia Department of Education

Contributing Writers

Rose-Marie Botting
Science Teacher
Broward County
   School District
Fort Lauderdale, Florida

Colleen Campos
Science Teacher
Laredo Middle School
Aurora, Colorado

Holly Estes
Science Teacher
Hale Middle School
Stow, Massachusetts

Edward Evans
Former Science
   Teacher
Hilton Central School
Hilton, New York

Sharon Stroud
Science Teacher
Widefield High School
Colorado Springs,
   Colorado

Reading Consultant

Bonnie B. Armbruster, Ph.D.
Department of Curriculum
   and Instruction
University of Illinois
Champaign, Illinois

Interdisciplinary Consultant

Heidi Hayes Jacobs, Ed.D.
Teacher's College
Columbia University
New York, New York

Safety Consultants

W. H. Breazeale, Ph.D.
Department of Chemistry
College of Charleston
Charleston, South Carolina

Ruth Hathaway, Ph.D.
Hathaway Consulting
Cape Girardeau, Missouri

Tufts University Program Reviewers

Content Reviewers

Teacher Reviewers

Stephanie Anderson
Sierra Vista Junior
    High School
Canyon Country, California

John W. Anson
Mesa Intermediate School
Palmdale, California

Pamela Arline
Lake Taylor Middle School
Norfolk, Virginia

Lynn Beason
College Station Jr. High School
College Station, Texas

Richard Bothmer
Hollis School District
Hollis, New Hampshire

Jeffrey C. Callister
Newburgh Free Academy
Newburgh, New York

Judy D'Albert
Harvard Day School
Corona Del Mar, California

Betty Scott Dean
Guilford County Schools
McLeansville, North Carolina

Sarah C. Duff
Baltimore City Public Schools
Baltimore, Maryland

Melody Law Ewey
Holmes Junior High School
Davis, California

Sherry L. Fisher
Lake Zurich Middle
    School North
Lake Zurich, Illinois

Melissa Gibbons
Fort Worth ISD
Fort Worth, Texas

Debra J. Goodding
Kraemer Middle School
Placentia, California

Jack Grande
Weber Middle School
Port Washington, New York

Steve Hills
Riverside Middle School
Grand Rapids, Michigan

Carol Ann Lionello
Kraemer Middle School
Placentia, California

Jaime A. Morales
Henry T. Gage Middle School
Huntington Park, California

Patsy Partin
Cameron Middle School
Nashville, Tennessee

Deedra H. Robinson
Newport News Public Schools
Newport News, Virginia

Bonnie Scott
Clack Middle School
Abilene, Texas

Charles M. Sears
Belzer Middle School
Indianapolis, Indiana

Barbara M. Strange
Ferndale Middle School
High Point, North Carolina

Jackie Louise Ulfig
Ford Middle School
Allen, Texas

Kathy Usina
Belzer Middle School
Indianapolis, Indiana

Heidi M. von Oetinger
L'Anse Creuse Public School
Harrison Township, Michigan

Pam Watson
Hill Country Middle School
Austin, Texas

Activity Field Testers

Nicki Bibbo
Russell Street School
Littleton, Massachusetts

Connie Boone
Fletcher Middle School
Jacksonville Beach, Florida

Rose-Marie Botting
Broward County
    School District
Fort Lauderdale, Florida

Colleen Campos
Laredo Middle School
Aurora, Colorado

Elizabeth Chait
W. L. Chenery Middle School
Belmont, Massachusetts

Holly Estes
Hale Middle School
Stow, Massachusetts

Laura Hapgood
Plymouth Community
    Intermediate School
Plymouth, Massachusetts

Sandra M. Harris
Winman Junior High School
Warwick, Rhode Island

Jason Ho
Walter Reed Middle School
Los Angeles, California

Joanne Jackson
Winman Junior High School
Warwick, Rhode Island

Mary F. Lavin
Plymouth Community
    Intermediate School
Plymouth, Massachusetts

James MacNeil, Ph.D.
Concord Public Schools
Concord, Massachusetts

Lauren Magruder
St. Michael's Country
    Day School
Newport, Rhode Island

Jeanne Maurand
Glen Urquhart School
Beverly Farms, Massachusetts

Warren Phillips
Plymouth Community
    Intermediate School
Plymouth, Massachusetts

Carol Pirtle
Hale Middle School
Stow, Massachusetts

Kathleen M. Poe
Kirby-Smith Middle School
Jacksonville, Florida

Cynthia B. Pope
Ruffner Middle School
Norfolk, Virginia

Anne Scammell
Geneva Middle School
Geneva, New York

Karen Riley Sievers
Callanan Middle School
Des Moines, Iowa

David M. Smith
Howard A. Eyer Middle School
Macungie, Pennsylvania

Derek Strohschneider
Plymouth Community
    Intermediate School
Plymouth, Massachusetts

Sallie Teames
Rosemont Middle School
Fort Worth, Texas

Gene Vitale
Parkland Middle School
McHenry, Illinois

Zenovia Young
Meyer Levin Junior
    High School (IS 285)
Brooklyn, New York

Contents

Earth's Changing Surface

Activities

Mammals of the JURASSIC PERIOD

Spending half your summer alone in a tiny trailer in a deserted part of Wyoming may not sound like fun. But for Kelli Trujillo, a graduate student in paleontology (pay lee un TAHL uh jee), it's a dream come true. As a paleontologist, she studies the remains of ancient living things.

Kelli Trujillo is working near Como Bluff, Wyoming, one of the most famous dinosaur graveyards in the United States. But she is not searching for dinosaur bones. Kelli is looking for the remains of mammals that lived during the late Jurassic Period, about 150 million years ago.

During the Jurassic Period, southeast Wyoming was flat and dotted with lakes and streams. The Rocky Mountains had not yet formed. Small animals lived in the shadows of the dinosaurs. Among these small animals were some of the earliest mammals: mouselike and shrewlike creatures. Very little is known about these mammals. Their bones are tiny, so finding them is difficult. "If I find a mammal tooth, that's a big deal, because those discoveries are still really rare," says Kelli.

Kelli Trujillo, 31, is a graduate student in vertebrate paleontology at the University of Wyoming. During the summer, she splits her time between several fossil digs. Kelli is a musician as well as an outdoor enthusiast. She plays guitar, flute, and piano.

Apatosaurus and small mammals lived in the same period.

Talking with Kelli Trujillo

Q *How did you get interested in science?*

A My dad was a history teacher, but he had a passion for geology, so we always had rocks around the house. We spent a lot of time outside, camping and hiking and looking at rocks. I knew what quartz and mica were before I even went to school.

Q *How did you choose geology?*

A In high school I took a geology class with a really great teacher who helped develop my interest, especially in fossils. But I didn't think I could be a geologist because you have to take algebra. Algebra was difficult for me. It scared me. So I got a degree in veterinary technology, which didn't require any math. I worked in that field for three years, but I just didn't like it. So I decided to go back to college and take the math classes I needed for a science degree.

Q *Why did you specialize in paleontology?*

A I got started as a volunteer on some fossil digs. The first was a student project near Gunnison, Colorado. A couple of students there had dug up more than 900 bone fragments from an *Apatosaurus,* a large four-legged dinosaur. Later, I helped a friend dig out an *Allosaurus,* a big meat-eating dinosaur, near Medicine Bow, Wyoming.

Q *What have you found at your fossil sites so far?*

A There are a lot of turtle shell fragments, about four or five square centimeters in size, with bumps and ridges in them. I've got lots of crocodile teeth and some lungfish teeth. I also have some salamander vertebrae—spinal column bones— and several vertebrae and jaw fragments from a small lizard called *Cteniogenys.* I've found twenty mammal teeth.

Q *How did those fragments happen to be preserved?*

A The animals probably lived in or near a small lake. When they died, their bodies got buried in sediments—layers of soil—at the bottom of the lake. The remains of these animals stayed buried for 150 million years.

Q *What can you infer about an organism from teeth or bone fragments?*

A You can usually tell a lot about animals from their teeth. That's because animals with different diets have different types of teeth. For instance, meat-eaters don't need grinding teeth like those that plant-eaters have. Crocodile and lizard teeth are pretty easy to identify. Mammal teeth are very specialized. In fact, these

Kelli looks for mammal fragments at this site in Wyoming (above). Kelli and a co-worker examine a fossil from the Jurassic Period (right).

◄ Kelli worked at some of the mammal and dinosaur sites located on this map.

KEY Dinosaur sites ■ Cities ●

specialized teeth are one of the things that separate mammals from other animals.

With bones, it really depends. If you have the entire bone, you can usually make a good guess about what type of animal it came from. But often you just find unidentifiable fragments.

Q *How does the rock where the fossil is found provide clues to the age of the fossil?*

A It's difficult to get an absolute age on sedimentary rocks. Often we just go by the rule that younger rocks are on top of older rocks. If we're really lucky, there will be a volcanic ash layer in the rocks, or certain crystals or iron minerals that we know how to date. In Wyoming, I'm working in a layer of rocks known as the Morrison Formation, which has been dated to the late Jurassic Period.

Q *How do scientists know where to dig for fossils?*

A Usually you see something on the surface, some scraps of bone sticking out from the rock. Bone has a different shape and texture and is often a different color. So if you know what you're looking for, a bone catches your eye.

Q *What tools do you use?*

A One of my most useful tools is a broom. I use it to clean the rocks so I can see their surfaces clearly. When you're digging out big bones, you use everything from picks and shovels to power tools like jackhammers and air drills. For small or delicate pieces, you need hand tools, like rock hammers and chisels, and a screen box. A screen box is basically a wooden box with a screen bottom. You put a couple of handfuls of rock in it and put the box

Dinosaur and Mammal Teeth

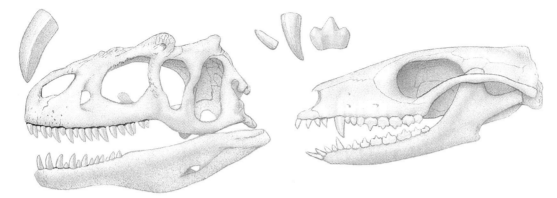

The strong jaws and long pointed teeth of *Allosaurus* (above) worked like a saw to tear apart smaller dinosaurs. *Allosaurus* was a large, meat-eating dinosaur of the Jurassic Period.

Mammal teeth are different from dinosaur teeth. The teeth of Jurassic mammals (above) are specialized for different functions. The combination of canines, incisors, and molars allowed the mammal to tear, shred, and grind.

←— Actual size of early mammal tooth

Actual size of *Allosaurus* tooth

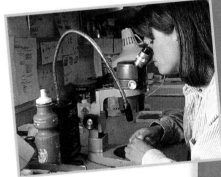

In her lab, Kelli uses her microscope to examine tiny mammal teeth.

in a big trough of water. You let the water wash the rock off the fossil. If you have the right kind of rock, it will wash away. But some rock never dissolves, and you're just out of luck.

Q *How do you recover the small mammal fossils?*

A I collect a couple of bags of rocks and bring them back to the lab. Then I wash them in the screen box, dry what's left, and search through it. The fossils are very small—some of them fit on the head of a pin! So you have to look at everything under a microscope, grain by grain, to see if you've got any fossils mixed in with the rock. It takes an awful lot of patience.

Q *What do you hope to find?*

A Usually teeth are all that's left of early mammals, but I'm hopeful this site will yield skulls and other bones, like arms or legs or vertebrae. I was

pretty excited when I found those twenty mammal teeth.

Q *Do you ever get discouraged or lonely out in the field?*

A When I'm out working at the site, the time goes so fast I don't even think about it. Being outside all day is wonderful. The bugs and wind aren't so good, but I'm in the middle of nowhere, and it's absolutely beautiful.

In Your Journal

Kelli Trujillo's work as a paleontologist involves a number of different steps. At each step, from searching a site for fossils to drawing conclusions in the lab, Kelli uses a wide range of skills. Make a two column list. In one column list the steps Kelli follows. In the second column describe the skills Kelli uses at each step.

WEB ACTIVITY
www.phschool.com

SECTION
1 **Exploring Earth's Surface**

Discover What Is the Land Like Around Your School?

SECTION
2 **Models of Earth**

Discover How Can You Flatten the Curved Earth?
Try This Where in the World?
Real-World Lab A Borderline Case

Integrating Technology 🌐
SECTION
3 **Maps in the Computer Age**

Discover Can You Make a Pixel Picture?

Getting on the Map

A shining river winds across a green plain. A plain is one of Earth's landforms. In this chapter, you will learn about plains and other landforms such as mountains and plateaus. You will also learn how to read and use maps that show the shape, height, and slope of Earth's surface. For this chapter project, you will select a small piece of land and draw a map of its physical features.

Your Goal To create a scale map of a small area of your neighborhood.

To complete this project you must
◆ work with your teacher or an adult family member
◆ choose and measure a small square or rectangular piece of land
◆ use a compass to locate north and draw a map to scale
◆ use symbols and a key to represent natural and human-made features of the land

Get Started Start looking for a suitable site. Your site should be about 300 to 1,000 square meters in area. It could be part of a park, playground, or backyard. Look for an area that includes interesting natural features such as trees, a stream, and changes in elevation or slope. There may be some human-made structures on your site, such as a park bench or sidewalk.

Check Your Progress You'll be working on this project as you study this chapter. To keep your project on track, look for Check Your Progress boxes at the following points.

Section 1 Review, page 18: Choose a site, measure the boundaries, and sketch all the physical features.
Section 2 Review, page 24: Brainstorm ideas for symbols to include on your map.
Section 4 Review, page 33: Complete the final draft of your map, including a key and map scale.

Wrap Up At the end of this chapter (page 37), you will present your map to the class.

The Cheyenne River flows through Buffalo Gap National Grassland near Red Shirt, South Dakota.

SECTION
4 **Topographic Maps**

Discover **Can a Map Show Relief?**
Sharpen Your Skills **Interpreting Data**
Skills Lab **A Map in a Pan**

SECTION 1 Exploring Earth's Surface

What Is the Land Like Around Your School?

1. On a piece of paper, draw a small square to represent your school.

2. Choose a word that describes the type of land near your school, such as flat, hilly, or rolling. Write the word next to the square.

3. Use a magnetic compass to determine the direction of north. Assume that north is at the top of your piece of paper.

4. If you travel due north 1 kilometer from your school, what type of land do you find? Choose a word to describe the land in this area. Write that word to the north of the square.

5. Repeat Step 4 for areas located 1 kilometer east, south, and west of your school.

Think It Over

Forming Operational Definitions What phrase could you use to describe the land in your area?

GUIDE FOR READING

◆ What determines the topography of Earth's surface?

◆ What are the main types of landforms?

◆ What are the four "spheres" that make up Earth's surface?

Reading Tip Before you read, preview *Exploring Landforms* on page 17. Make a list of questions you have about landforms.

In 1804, an expedition set out from St. Louis to explore the land between the Mississippi River and the Pacific Ocean. The United States had just purchased a part of this vast territory, called Louisiana, from France. Before the Louisiana Purchase, the United States stretched from the Atlantic coast westward to the Mississippi River. Few United States citizens had traveled west of the Mississippi. None had ever traveled over land all the way to the Pacific.

Led by Meriwether Lewis and William Clark, the expedition traveled up the Missouri River, crossed the Rocky Mountains, followed the Columbia River to the Pacific Ocean—and then returned. The purpose of the expedition was to map America's interior and discover resources.

Topography

On the journey to the Pacific, the Lewis and Clark expedition traveled more than 5,000 kilometers across the continent of North America. As they traveled, Lewis and Clark observed many changes in topography. **Topography** is the shape of the land. An area's topography may be flat, sloping, hilly, or mountainous.

Figure 1 While traveling down the Columbia River, the Lewis and Clark expedition meets the Chinook people.

The topography of an area is determined by the area's elevation, relief, and landforms. The desktop where you do homework probably has piles of books, papers, and other objects of different sizes and shapes. Your desktop has both elevation and relief!

Elevation The height above sea level of a point on Earth's surface is its **elevation.** When Lewis and Clark started in St. Louis, they were about 140 meters above sea level. By the time they reached Lemhi Pass in the Rocky Mountains, they were more than 2,200 meters above sea level.

Relief The difference in elevation between the highest and lowest parts of an area is its **relief.** As the Lewis and Clark expedition entered the Rocky Mountains, the relief of the land changed from flat or rolling land with low relief to huge mountains with high relief.

Landforms If you followed the route of the Lewis and Clark expedition, you would see many different landforms. A **landform** is a feature of topography formed by the processes that shape Earth's surface. All landforms have elevation and relief. A large area of land where the topography is similar is called a **landform region.** Figure 3 shows the landform regions of the United States not including Alaska or Hawaii.

☑ *Checkpoint* *What is the difference between elevation and relief?*

KEY
← Route of Lewis and Clark, west
→ Route of Lewis and Clark, east
  Louisiana Purchase
  United States in 1803

Figure 2 The Lewis and Clark expedition followed major rivers, except when crossing the Rocky Mountains.

Figure 3 The United States has many different landform regions. *Interpreting Maps In what regions are Charleston, Topeka, Santa Fe, and Walla Walla located?*

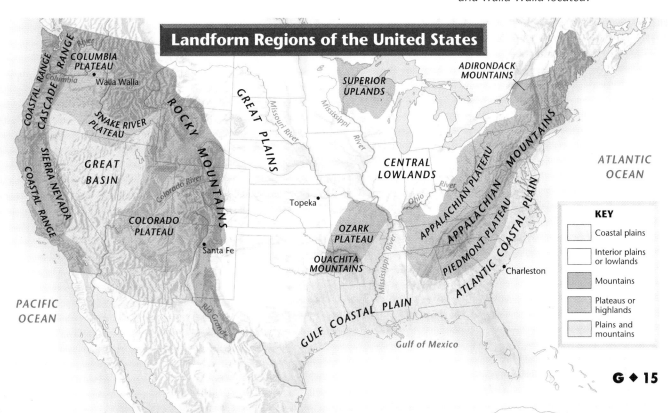

Landform Regions of the United States

KEY
  Coastal plains
  Interior plains or lowlands
  Mountains
  Plateaus or highlands
  Plains and mountains

Figure 4 The Great Plains of western North America include a vast area of flat or rolling land. The Great Plains are interior plains. *Predicting What do you think would be some differences between interior plains and coastal plains?*

Types of Landforms

Landforms can vary greatly in size and shape—from level plains extending as far as the eye can see, to low, rounded hills that you could climb on foot, to jagged mountains that would take you days to walk around. **There are three main types of landforms: plains, mountains, and plateaus.**

Plains A **plain** is a landform made up of flat or gently rolling land with low relief. A plain that lies along a seacoast is called a coastal plain. In North America, a coastal plain wraps like an apron around the continent's eastern and southeastern shores. Coastal plains have both low elevation and low relief.

A plain that lies away from the coast is called an interior plain. Although interior plains have low relief, their elevation can vary. The broad interior plain of North America is called the Great Plains.

The Great Plains extend from Texas north into Canada. From their eastern border in the states of North and South Dakota, Nebraska, Kansas, Oklahoma, and Texas, the Great Plains stretch west to the Rocky Mountains. At the time of the Lewis and Clark expedition, the Great Plains were a vast grassland.

Figure 5 The Bitterroot Mountains in Idaho are part of the Rocky Mountains system.

Mountains A **mountain** is a landform with high elevation and high relief. Mountains usually occur as part of a mountain range. A **mountain range** is a group of mountains that are closely related in shape, structure, and age. After crossing the Great Plains, the Lewis and Clark expedition crossed a rugged mountain range in Idaho called the Bitterroot Mountains.

The different mountain ranges in a region make up a mountain system. The Bitterroot Mountains are one mountain range in the mountain system known as the Rocky Mountains.

Mountain ranges and mountain systems in a long, connected chain form a larger unit called a mountain belt. The Rocky Mountains are part of a great mountain belt that stretches down the western sides of North America and South America.

Plateaus A landform that has high elevation and a more or less level surface is called a **plateau**. A plateau is rarely perfectly smooth on top. Streams and rivers may cut into the plateau's surface. The Columbia Plateau in Washington State is an example. The Columbia River, which the Lewis and Clark expedition followed, slices through this plateau. The many layers of rock that make up the Columbia Plateau are about 1,500 meters thick.

☑ *Checkpoint* *What types of landforms have low relief?*

EXPLORING *Landforms*

Mountains, plains, and plateaus are just a few of the many landforms that make up the topography of Earth's surface.

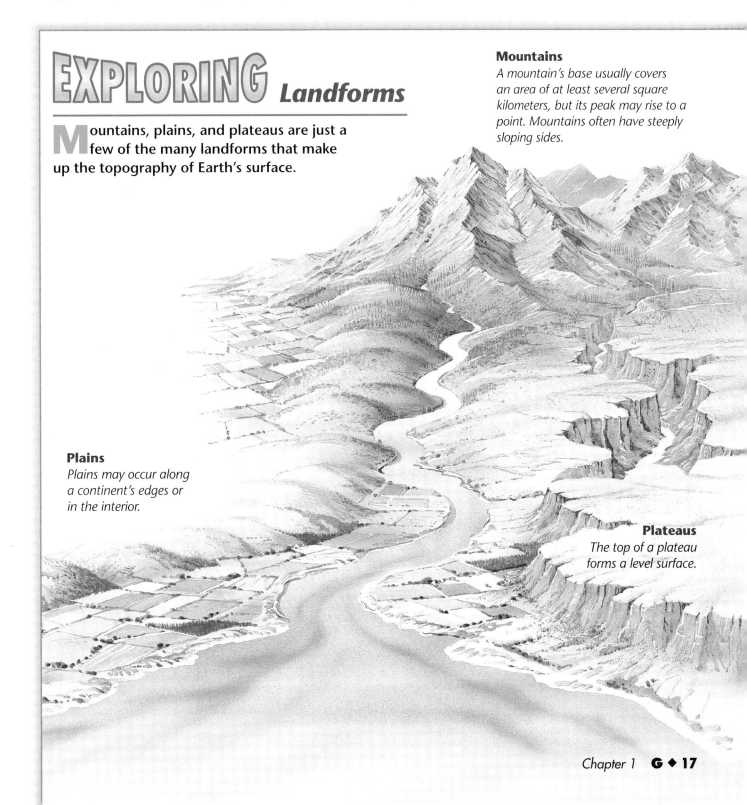

Mountains
A mountain's base usually covers an area of at least several square kilometers, but its peak may rise to a point. Mountains often have steeply sloping sides.

Plains
Plains may occur along a continent's edges or in the interior.

Plateaus
The top of a plateau forms a level surface.

Earth's Four Spheres

Lewis and Clark's two-year journey took them across western North America. Along the way, they observed the land, water, air, and living things. Together, these four things make up everything that is on and around planet Earth. **Scientists divide Earth into four spheres: the lithosphere, hydrosphere, atmosphere, and biosphere.** In this book, you will learn mainly about the lithosphere and how it is affected by each of the other spheres.

Earth's solid, rocky outer layer is called the **lithosphere** (LITH uh sfeer). The lithosphere is made up of the continents as well as smaller landmasses called islands. The lithosphere extends under the entire ocean floor. The surface of the lithosphere varies from smooth plains to wrinkled hills and valleys to jagged mountain peaks.

The outermost sphere is the **atmosphere** (AT muh sfeer), the mixture of gases that surrounds the planet. By far the most abundant gases are nitrogen and oxygen, but the atmosphere also contains water vapor, carbon dioxide, and other gases. When water vapor condenses, it forms the droplets that make up clouds.

Earth's oceans, lakes, rivers, and ice form the **hydrosphere** (HY druh sfeer). Most of the hydrosphere consists of the salt water in the oceans, but fresh water is also part of the hydrosphere. Oceans cover more than two thirds of Earth.

All living things—whether in the air, in the oceans, or on and beneath the land surface—make up the **biosphere** (BY uh sfeer). The biosphere extends into each of the other spheres.

Figure 6 A view from space shows all four of Earth's spheres—the atmosphere, hydrosphere, biosphere, and lithosphere. *Observing What evidence of each of the spheres can you see in the photograph?*

Section 1 Review

1. What three factors determine the topography of a region?
2. What are the most common types of landforms?
3. Which is larger, a mountain belt or a mountain system?
4. In which of Earth's spheres would you find a cloud? A mountain? A lake? A tree?
5. **Thinking Critically Comparing and Contrasting** How are mountains and plateaus similar? How are they different?

Check Your Progress

CHAPTER PROJECT 1

Choose a site that is as square or rectangular as possible. **CAUTION:** *Make sure to obtain permission from the property owner before you begin.* To start mapping your site, mark the four corners with stakes, stones, or other markers. Measure the boundaries and record the distances on a rough sketch. Your sketch should show your site's topography, plus natural and human-made features. Include a north arrow on your sketch. How can you determine which direction is north?

SECTION
2 Models of Earth

DISCOVER · ACTIVITY

How Can You Flatten the Curved Earth?

1. Using a felt-tip pen, make a rough sketch of the outlines of the continents on the surface of an orange or grapefruit.

2. ✂ Using a plastic knife, carefully peel the orange. If possible, keep the peel in one large piece so that the continents remain intact.

3. Try to lay the pieces of orange peel flat on a table.

Think It Over

Observing What happens to the continents when you try to flatten the pieces? What adjustments would you need to make to the shapes of the continents to get them to match their shape and position on a sphere?

You want to invite relatives from out of town to a sports event at your school. You could use words to explain how to find the school: Take the third exit off the highway, turn left at the first traffic light, and so on. But verbal directions can be hard to follow. Instead, you might sketch a map of the best route to your school. Maps use a picture instead of words to tell where things are.

Maps and Globes

Maps and globes show the shape, size, and position of Earth's surface features. A **map** is a model on a flat surface of all or part of Earth's surface as seen from above. A **globe** is a sphere that represents Earth's entire surface. A globe correctly shows the relative size and shape of landmasses and bodies of water, much as if you were viewing Earth from space.

Maps and globes are drawn to scale and use symbols to represent topography and other features on Earth's surface. A map's **scale** relates distance on a map to a distance on Earth's surface. Scale is often given as a ratio. For example, one unit on the map equals 25,000 units on the ground. So one centimeter on the map represents 0.25 kilometers. This scale, "one to twenty-five thousand," would be written "1 : 25,000." Figure 7 shows three ways of giving a map's scale.

GUIDE FOR READING

◆ How do maps and globes represent Earth's surface?

◆ How are latitude and longitude used to locate points on Earth's surface?

Reading Tip Before you read, rewrite the headings in the section as *how, why,* or *what* questions. As you read, look for answers to these questions.

Figure 7 Here are three ways to show scale on a map.

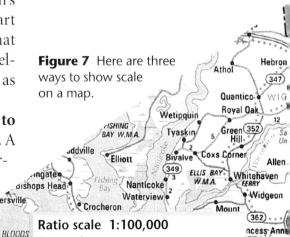

Ratio scale 1:100,000
Bar scale

0	1	2	3	4	5 km

0	1	2	3 mi

Equivalent units scale
1 cm = 1 km   1 inch = 1.58 miles

Mapmakers use pictures called **symbols** to stand for features on Earth's surface. A symbol can represent a physical feature, such as a river, lake, mountain, or plain. A symbol also can stand for a human-made feature, such as a highway, a city, or an airport. A map's **key,** or legend, is a list of all the symbols used on the map with an explanation of their meaning.

Maps also include a compass rose or north arrow. The compass rose helps the map user to relate directions on the map to directions on Earth's surface. North usually is located at the top of the map.

☑ *Checkpoint* *Where can you find the meaning of the symbols on a map?*

Maps and Technology

Centuries ago, people invented instruments for determining compass direction, latitude, and longitude. Mapmakers developed techniques to show Earth's surface accurately.

1154 Sicily

The Arab mapmaker Al-Idrisi made several world maps for King Roger of Sicily. Idrisi's maps marked a great advance over other maps of that time. They showed the Arabs' grasp of scientific mapmaking and geography. But unlike modern maps, these maps placed south at the top!

| 1100 | 1200 | 1300 | 1400 |

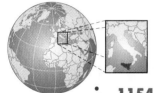

AROUND 1100 China

Because the needle of a magnetic compass points north, ships at sea could tell direction even when the sun and stars were not visible. Arabs and Europeans adopted this Chinese invention by the 1200s.

AROUND 1300 Spain

Lines representing wind directions criss-crossed a type of map called a portolan chart. These charts also showed coastlines and harbors. A sea captain would use a portolan chart and a compass when sailing from one harbor to another in the Mediterranean Sea.

An Earth Reference System

When you play chess or checkers, the grid of squares helps you to keep track of where each piece should be. To find a point on Earth's surface, you need a reference system like the grid of squares on a checkerboard. Of course, Earth itself does not have grid lines, but most maps and globes show a grid. The grid is based on two imaginary lines: the equator and the prime meridian.

The Equator Halfway between the North and South poles, the **equator** forms an imaginary line that circles Earth. The equator divides Earth into the Northern and Southern hemispheres. A **hemisphere** (HEH mih sfeer) is one half of the sphere that makes up Earth's surface.

In Your Journal

Choose one period on the time line to learn more about. Use the library to find information about maps in that time. Who used maps? Why were they important? Share what you learn in the form of a letter written by a traveler or explorer who is using a map of that period.

1595 England

To find latitude, sailors used a variety of instruments, including the backstaff. The navigator sighted along the backstaff's straight edge to measure the angle of the sun or North star above the horizon. Later improvements led to modern instruments for navigation.

1684 France

On land, mapmakers developed new ways of measuring land areas accurately. Philippe de La Hire's map of France proved that the country was actually smaller than people had thought. The king of France said that he lost more land because of this map than he would have lost through losing a war.

1500	1600	1700	1800

1569 Belgium

Flemish mapmaker Gerardus Mercator invented the first modern map projection, which bears his name. Mercator and his son, Rumold, also made an atlas and maps of the world such as the one shown below.

1763 England

John Harrison, a carpenter and mechanic, won a prize from the British navy for building a highly accurate clock called a chronometer. Harrison's invention made finding longitudes quicker and easier. With exact longitudes, mapmakers could greatly improve the accuracy of their maps.

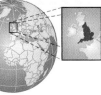
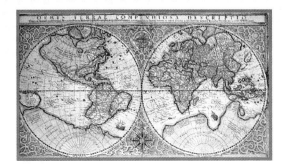

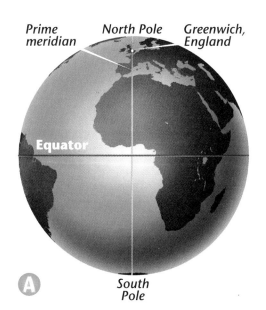

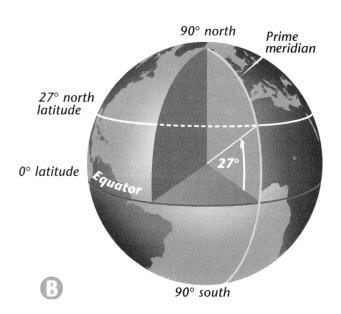

Figure 8 A. The equator and the prime meridian divide Earth's surface into hemispheres.
B. Latitude measures distances north or south of the equator.
C. Longitude measures distances east or west of the prime meridian.
D. Cairo, Egypt, is located where the latitude line 30° N crosses the longitude line 31° E.

Where in the World?

Using a globe, determine what city is found at each of the following points:

    2° S 79° W
    38° N 9° W
    34° N 135° E
    34° S 58° W
    55° N 3° W
    1° N 103° E

What word is spelled by the first letters of these city names?

The Prime Meridian Another imaginary line, called the **prime meridian,** makes a half circle from the North Pole to the South Pole. The prime meridian passes through Greenwich, England. Places east of the prime meridian are in the Eastern Hemisphere. Places west of the prime meridian are in the Western Hemisphere.

Measurements on a Sphere To measure distances around a circle, scientists use units called degrees. A **degree** (°) is $\frac{1}{360}$ of the way around a full circle. As you can see in Figure 8, each degree is a measure of the angle formed by lines drawn from the center of Earth to points on the surface. If you started at the prime meridian and traveled west along the equator, you would travel through 360 degrees before returning to your starting point. If you started at the equator and traveled to one of the poles, you would travel 90 degrees—one quarter of the distance in a full circle.

Checkpoint *In what two hemispheres is the United States located?*

Locating Points on Earth's Surface

Using the equator and prime meridian, mapmakers have constructed a grid made up of lines of latitude and longitude. **You can use lines of latitude and longitude to find locations anywhere on Earth.**

Latitude The equator is the starting line for measuring **latitude,** or distance in degrees north or south of the equator. Between the equator and both poles are evenly spaced lines called lines of latitude. All lines of latitude are parallel to the equator. Latitude is measured from the equator, which is at 0°. The latitude of each pole is 90° north or 90° south.

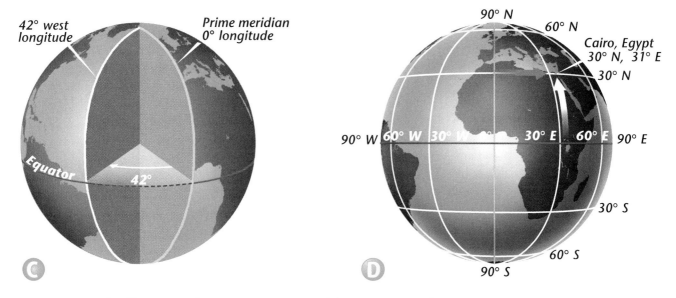

Longitude The distance in degrees east or west of the prime meridian is called **longitude.** There are 360 lines of longitude that run from north to south, meeting at the poles. Each line represents one degree of longitude. The prime meridian, which is the starting line for measuring longitude, is at 0°. Each longitude line crosses the latitude lines, including the equator, at a right angle.

As Figure 9 shows, the longitude lines in each hemisphere are numbered up to 180 degrees. This is one half the total number of degrees in a circle. At 180 degrees east or 180 degrees west lies a single longitude line directly opposite the prime meridian.

Figure 9 Every point on Earth's surface has a particular latitude and longitude. *Interpreting Maps What are the latitude and longitude of New Orleans? Of Sydney?*

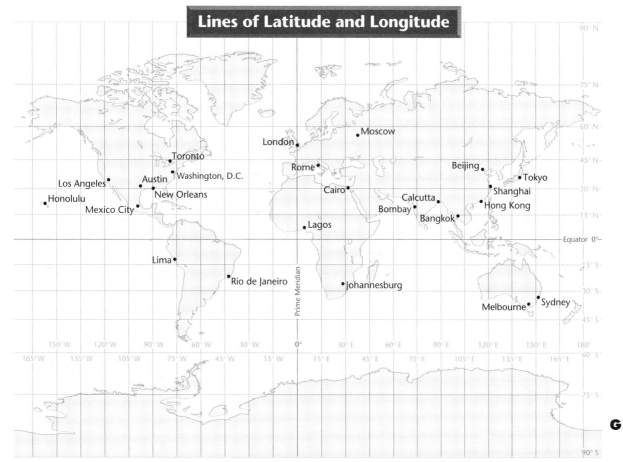

Lines of Latitude and Longitude

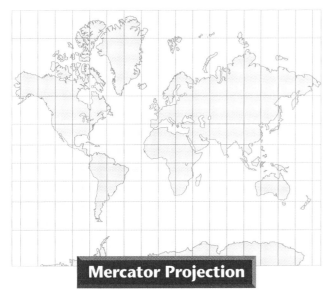

Mercator Projection

Equal-Area Projection

Figure 10 On a Mercator projection (left), lines of longitude are parallel, so shapes near the poles are distorted. An equal-area projection (right) shows areas correctly, but distorts some shapes around its edges.
Comparing and Contrasting Why does Greenland appear larger on the Mercator projection than on the equal-area projection?

Map Projections

To show Earth's curved surface on a flat map, mapmakers use map projections. A **map projection** is a framework of lines that helps to show landmasses on a flat surface.

On a Mercator projection, the lines of latitude and longitude all appear as straight, parallel lines that form a rectangle. On a Mercator projection, the size and shape of landmasses near the equator are distorted only a little. But as you go toward the poles, size and shape become more and more distorted. The reason for this distortion is that the lines of longitude do not come together at the poles as they do on a globe. As you can see in Figure 10, this projection also changes the relative sizes of landmasses.

To solve the problem of distortion on Mercator projections, mapmakers developed equal-area projections. An equal-area projection correctly shows the relative sizes of Earth's landmasses. But an equal-area projection also has distortion. The shapes of landmasses near the edges of the map appear stretched and curved.

 Section 2 Review

1. What information does a map's scale provide?
2. What do latitude and longitude each measure?
3. What are the advantages and disadvantages of an equal-area projection?
4. **Thinking Critically Measuring** Look at the map in Figure 9. If you fly due east from New Orleans, through how many degrees of longitude must you travel to reach Shanghai? If you flew west from New Orleans, how many degrees of longitude would you pass before reaching Shanghai? Explain.

Check Your Progress

CHAPTER PROJECT 1

Choose an appropriate scale for your map. Make a list of the types of natural and human-made features for which you will need symbols. Examine the samples of maps in the chapter and those provided by your teacher. Brainstorm ideas for symbols to include. If possible, return to your site and add more detail to your map.

A **Borderline** *Case*

You may have wondered how people first decided where to locate the borders between states.

Problem

Which was more important in locating state borders: lines of latitude and longitude or physical features?

Skills Focus

drawing conclusions, observing, inferring

Materials

United States map with latitude, longitude, and state borders
tracing paper   paper clips   colored pencils

Procedure

1. Lay a sheet of tracing paper on top of a map of the United States.
2. Trace over the Pacific and Atlantic coasts of the United States with a blue pencil.
3. Using the blue pencil, trace all Great Lakes shorelines that reach nearby states.
4. Trace all state borders that go exactly north-south with a red pencil. (*Hint:* Some straight-line borders that appear to run north-south, such as the western border of Maine, do not follow lines of longitude.)
5. Use a green pencil to trace all state borders or sections of state borders that go exactly east-west. (*Hint:* Straight-line borders that are slanted, such as the southern border of Nevada, do not follow lines of latitude.)

6. Now use a blue pencil to trace the borders that follow rivers.
7. Use a brown pencil to trace any borders that are not straight lines or rivers.

Analyze and Conclude

1. How many state boundaries are completely defined by longitude and latitude? How many are partially defined by longitude and latitude?
2. What feature is used to define a state border when longitude and latitude are not used? Give examples of specific states.
3. Study the physical map of the United States in Appendix B. What other physical features are used to define borders? Which state borders are defined by these features?
4. Which was used more often in locating state borders: longitude or latitude?
5. How many states do not use longitude and latitude for the location of their borders?
6. **Apply** In which region of the country were lines of latitude and longitude most important in determining state borders? What do you think is the reason for this?

More to Explore

Research the history of your state to find out when and how its borders were established. Are your state's borders based on longitude and latitude, landforms and topography, or both?

Review a map of your county or state. Are any features, other than the state's border, related to longitude and latitude? Which features seem to follow landforms and topography?

SECTION 3 Maps in the Computer Age

DISCOVER •••ACTIVITY••••

Can You Make a Pixel Picture?

1. With a pencil, draw a square grid of lines spaced 1 centimeter apart. The grid should have 6 squares on each side.

2. On the grid, draw the outline of a simple object, such as an apple.

3. Using a different color pencil, fill in all squares that are completely inside the apple. If a square is mostly inside the apple, fill it in completely. If it is mostly outside, leave it blank.

4. Each square on your grid represents one pixel, or bit of information, about your picture. Looking at your pixel picture, can you recognize the shape you started with?

Think It Over

Predicting How would the pixel picture change if you drew the object smaller? How would the pixel picture look if you used graph paper with squares that are smaller than your grid?

GUIDE FOR READING

◆ How are satellites and computers used in mapmaking?

Reading Tip Before you read, preview Figures 12 and 13. In your notebook, describe how you think computers may have affected mapmaking.

Figure 11 A satellite image is made up of many pixels. This enlargement of a satellite image shows Tampa Bay and St. Petersburg, Florida.

For centuries, mapmakers slowly gathered data and then drew maps by hand. Explorers made maps by sketching coastlines as seen from their ships. Mapmakers sometimes drew the land based on reports from people who had traveled there. More accurate maps were made by locating points on the surface in a process called surveying.

During the twentieth century, people learned to make highly accurate maps using photographs taken from airplanes. These photographs are called aerial photographs. Aerial photographs are still important in many types of mapmaking.

Since the 1970s, information gathered by satellites has revolutionized mapmaking. Powerful computers use the satellite data to make maps quickly and accurately.

Satellite Mapping

Beginning in 1972, the United States launched a series of Landsat satellites designed to observe Earth's surface. Landsat uses electronic devices to collect information about the land surface in the form of computer data. **Satellite images** are pictures of the surface based on these data. As Landsat orbits Earth, it collects and stores information about a strip of the surface that is

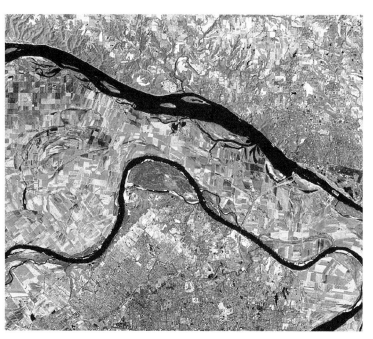

185 kilometers wide. The satellite relays the data back to a station on Earth, where computers create images of the surface.

Pictures made by Landsat show what covers the land surface—plants, soil, sand, rock, water, or snow and ice. Large human-made features, such as cities, are also visible.

Printing Satellite Images Unlike a photograph, a satellite image is made up of thousands of tiny dots called **pixels.** A painting made of pixels would have many separate dots of color. Each pixel in a satellite image contains information on the color and brightness of a small part of Earth's surface. This information is stored on a computer as a series of 0's and 1's. When the satellite image is printed, the computer translates these numbers into colors.

Interpreting Satellite Images Scientists learn to identify

INTEGRATING specific features by the "signa-
ENVIRONMENTAL SCIENCE ture," or combination of colors

and shapes, that the feature makes on a satellite image. In a satellite image, areas covered by grass, trees, or crops are often shown as red, water as black or blue, and cities as bluish gray. Landsat images may show features such as grasslands, forests, and agricultural crops, as well as desert areas, mountains, or cities. By comparing one image with another made at an earlier time, scientists can see changes due to drought, forest fires, or floods. Figure 12 shows satellite images taken before and during a flood in the Mississippi River valley.

☑ *Checkpoint* *What information does a pixel in a satellite image contain?*

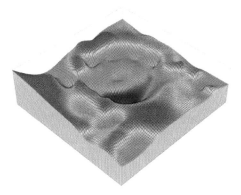

Figure 13 Today computers are an essential tool in making accurate maps. A computer produced the digital model shown above.

Computer Mapping

With computers, mapmakers have new ways of storing and displaying map data. Computer mapmakers use up-to-the-minute data to produce maps quickly and easily.

All of the data used in computer mapping must be in numbers, just like the pixels in a satellite image. The process by which mapmakers convert the location of map points to numbers is called **digitizing.** Once the map data have been digitized, they can be displayed on a computer screen, modified, and printed out in map form.

Computers can automatically create three-dimensional views that might take a person hundreds of hours to draw by hand. The computer image in Figure 13, for example, was made to help geologists search for oil.

Section 3 Review

1. Describe how Landsat collects data about Earth's surface.
2. What are the two ways in which computers are useful in making maps?
3. How are the data for a map put in a form that a computer can use?
4. **Thinking Critically Making Generalizations** In your own words, describe how computers and satellites have improved the accuracy of maps.

Science at Home

Most of the maps that you see today in newspapers and magazines are made using computers. With family members look through newspapers and news magazines. How many different types of maps can you find? Explain to your family the map's scale, symbols, and key. After you have studied the map, try to state the main point of the information shown on the map.

SECTION 4 Topographic Maps

DISCOVER .... ACTIVITY

Can a Map Show Relief?

1. ✂ Carefully cut the corners off 8 pieces of cardboard so that they look rounded. Each piece should be at least 1 centimeter smaller than the one before.

2. Trim the long sides of the two largest pieces so that the long sides appear wavy. Don't cut any more than one-half centimeter into the cardboard.

3. Trace the largest cardboard piece on a sheet of paper.

4. Trace the next largest piece inside the tracing of the first. Don't let any lines cross.

5. Trace the other cardboard pieces, from largest to smallest, one inside the other, on the same paper.

6. Stack the cardboard pieces in the same order they were traced beside the paper. Compare the stack of cardboard pieces with your drawing. How are they alike? How are they different?

Think It Over

Making Models If the cardboard pieces are a model of a landform, what do the lines on the paper represent?

Y ou are an engineer planning a route for a highway over a mountain pass. You need to consider many different factors. To design a safe highway, you need a route that avoids the steepest slopes. To protect the area's water supply, the highway must stay a certain distance from rivers and lakes. You also want to find a route that avoids houses and other buildings. How would you find the best route? You could start by studying a topographic map.

Mapping Earth's Topography

A **topographic map** is a map showing the surface features of an area. Topographic maps use symbols to portray the land as if you were looking down on it from above. **Topographic maps provide highly accurate information on the elevation, relief, and slope of the ground surface.**

GUIDE FOR READING

◆ What is a topographic map?

◆ How do mapmakers represent elevation, relief, and slope?

◆ What is the Global Positioning System?

Reading Tip As you read, make a list of main ideas and supporting details about topographic maps.

Figure 14 Topographic maps provide the data necessary for the planning of highways, bridges, and other large construction projects.

Math TOOLBOX

Scale and Ratios

A ratio compares two numbers by division. For example, the scale of a map given as a ratio is 1 : 250,000. At this scale, the distance between two points on the map measures 23.5 cm. How would you find the actual distance? Begin by writing the scale as a fraction.

$$\frac{1}{250,000}$$

Next, write a proportion. Let d represent the actual distance between the two points.

$$\frac{1}{250,000} = \frac{23.5 \text{ cm}}{d}$$

Then write the cross products.

$$1 \times d = 250,000 \times 23.5 \text{ cm}$$
$$d = 5,875,000 \text{ cm}$$

(*Hint:* To convert cm to km, divide d by 100,000.)

Uses of Topographic Maps People find many uses for topographic maps. Businesses use them to help decide where to build new stores, housing, or factories. Cities and towns use them to decide where to build new schools. Topographic maps have recreational uses, too. If you were planning a bicycle trip, you could use a topographic map to see whether your trip would be flat or hilly.

Scale Topographic maps usually are large-scale maps. A large-scale map is one that shows a close-up view of part of Earth's surface. In the United States, most topographic maps are at a scale of 1 : 24,000, or 1 centimeter equals 0.24 kilometers. At this scale, a map can show the details of elevation and features such as rivers and coastlines. Large buildings, airports, and major highways appear as outlines at the correct scale. Symbols are used to show houses and other small features.

Coverage Most nations have a government agency that is responsible for making topographic maps. In the United States, that agency is the U. S. Geological Survey, or USGS. The USGS has produced about 57,000 topographic maps at scales of either 1 : 24,000 or 1 : 25,000. The maps cover all of the United States, except for parts of Alaska. Each map covers an area of roughly 145 square kilometers.

Symbols Mapmakers use a great variety of symbols on topographic maps. If you were drawing a map, what symbols would you use to represent woods, a campground, an orchard, a swamp, or a school? Look at Figure 15 to see the symbols that the USGS uses for these and other features.

☑ *Checkpoint* *In the United States, what agency is responsible for producing topographic maps?*

Figure 15 Maps made by the U. S. Geological Survey use more than 150 symbols.

Commonly Used Map Symbols

Contour line: elevation	⬭	Primary highway	▬▬	River	〜
Contour line: depression	⬭	Secondary highway	▬ ▬	Stream	~
Building	■ □ ▨ ▨	Divided highway	▬▬	Waterfall or rapids	
School; church	⚑ ✝	Railroad tracks	╪╪╪╪	Marsh or swamp	
Built-up area		Airport	✕	Rock or coral reef	Reef
Campground; picnic area	⛺ ⊼	Woods		Breakwater; wharf	
Cemetery	⌐Cem¬	Orchard		Exposed wreck	

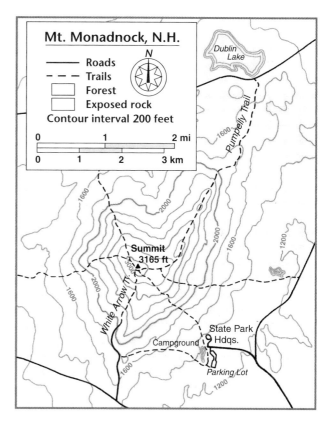

Figure 16 The contour lines on a topographic map represent elevation and relief. *Comparing and Contrasting What information does the topographic map provide that the photograph does not?*

Showing Relief on Topographic Maps

To represent elevation, relief, and slope on topographic maps, mapmakers use contour lines. On a topographic map, a **contour line** connects points of equal elevation.

The change in elevation from contour line to contour line is called the **contour interval.** The contour interval for a given map is always the same. For example, the map in Figure 16 has a contour interval of 200 feet. If you start at one contour line and count up 10 contour lines, you have reached an elevation 2,000 feet above where you started. Usually, every fifth contour line is darker and heavier than the others. These lines are labeled with the elevation in round units, such as 1,600 or 2,000 feet above sea level. Most USGS maps give contour intervals in feet rather than meters.

Looking at a topographic map with many squiggly contour lines, you may feel as if you are gazing into a bowl of spaghetti. But if you follow the rules listed in *Exploring Topographic Maps* on the following page, you can learn to read contour lines. Reading contour lines is the first step toward "seeing" an area's topography by looking at a topographic map.

Interpreting Data

You are planning to hike up Mt. Monadnock. Use the topographic map in Figure 16 to determine which route is steeper: the White Arrow Trail or the Pumpelly Trail. What is the difference in elevation between the park headquarters and the summit?

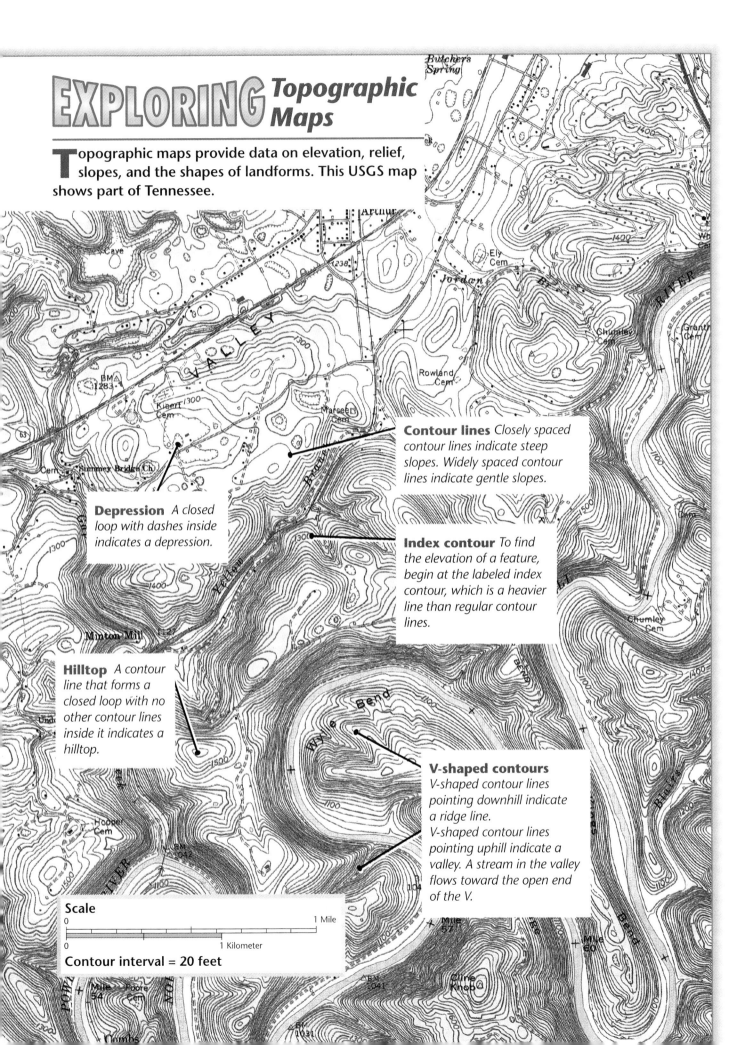

EXPLORING Topographic Maps

Topographic maps provide data on elevation, relief, slopes, and the shapes of landforms. This USGS map shows part of Tennessee.

Contour lines *Closely spaced contour lines indicate steep slopes. Widely spaced contour lines indicate gentle slopes.*

Depression *A closed loop with dashes inside indicates a depression.*

Index contour *To find the elevation of a feature, begin at the labeled index contour, which is a heavier line than regular contour lines.*

Hilltop *A contour line that forms a closed loop with no other contour lines inside it indicates a hilltop.*

V-shaped contours *V-shaped contour lines pointing downhill indicate a ridge line. V-shaped contour lines pointing uphill indicate a valley. A stream in the valley flows toward the open end of the V.*

Scale

0   1 Mile

0   1 Kilometer

Contour interval = 20 feet

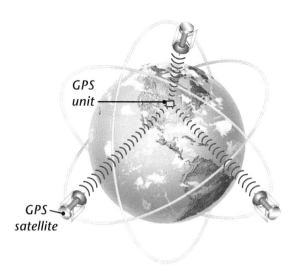

GPS unit

GPS satellite

Figure 17 The GPS network includes 24 satellites. Three satellites (left) must be above the horizon to pinpoint the location of the user (right). The user's latitude and longitude appear on the screen of a portable GPS unit like the one in the photograph.

Global Positioning System

INTEGRATING TECHNOLOGY Today, surveyors, pilots, and mapmakers around the world rely on the **Global Positioning System,** or GPS, to determine locations precisely. **The Global Positioning System is a method of finding latitude, longitude, and elevation of points on Earth's surface using a network of satellites.** At any given moment, there are between five and eight GPS satellites above the horizon in a given area. A hand-held unit the size of a cellular phone picks up signals broadcast by these satellites. A computer inside the GPS unit then calculates the user's location and elevation.

Engineers can use GPS to locate points on the ground for a construction project. Airplanes, ships, and hikers can use GPS to navigate. Some cars now contain both a GPS unit and a digital road map stored in a computer. Using GPS, the computer determines the car's location and suggests a route to your destination.

Section 4 Review

1. What kind of information does a topographic map provide about landforms?
2. How do topographic maps represent elevation and relief?
3. What would the highest and lowest points in an area look like on a topographic map?
4. What is the role of satellites in the Global Positioning System?
5. **Thinking Critically Interpreting Maps** Look at the map on page 32. Where is the highest elevation? Where do you find the steepest slopes? The gentlest slopes?

Check Your Progress

CHAPTER PROJECT 1

On a large piece of paper, draw your map to scale. Locate all natural and human-made features on the map using the measurements you recorded on your rough sketch and the symbols you brainstormed earlier. Include a north arrow, a legend, and scale on your map. Show the topography of the land by using contour lines or other symbols that show how the land slopes. ·

Making Models

A Map in a Pan

A topographic map is a two-dimensional model of three-dimensional landforms.

Problem

How can you make a topographic map?

Materials

deep-sided pan
marking pencil
clear, hard sheet of plastic
sheet of unlined white paper

water
modeling clay
metric ruler
food coloring

Procedure

1. Place a lump of clay on the bottom of a deep-sided pan. Shape the clay into a model of a hill.
2. Pour colored water into the pan to a depth of 1 centimeter to represent sea level.
3. Place a sheet of hard, clear plastic over the container.
4. Trace the outline of the pan on the plastic sheet with a marking pencil. Then, looking straight down into the pan, trace the outline the water makes around the edges of the clay model. Remove the plastic sheet from the pan.

5. Add another centimeter of water to the pan, bringing the depth of the water to 2 centimeters. Replace the plastic sheet exactly as before, then trace the water level again.
6. Repeat Step 5 several times. Stop when the next addition of water would completely cover your model.
7. Remove the plastic sheet. Trace the outlines that you drew on the plastic sheet onto a sheet of paper.

Analyze and Conclude

1. Looking at your topographic map, how can you tell which parts of your model hill have a steep slope? A gentle slope?
2. How can you tell from the map which point on the hill is the highest?
3. Where on your map would you be likely to find a stream? Explain.
4. Is there any depression on your map where water would collect after it rained? What symbol should you use to identify this depression?
5. **Think About It** Compare your map with the clay landform. How are they alike? How are they different? How could you improve your map as a model of the landform?

More to Explore

Obtain a topographic map that includes an interesting landform such as a mountain, canyon, river valley, or coastline. After studying the contour lines on the map, make a sketch of what you think the landform looks like. Then build a scale model of the landform using clay or layers of cardboard or foamboard. How does your model landform compare with your sketch?

SECTION 1 Exploring Earth's Surface

Key Ideas
◆ Earth's topography is made up of landforms that have elevation and relief, such as plains, mountains, and plateaus.
◆ The atmosphere, hydrosphere, and biosphere surround Earth's rocky outer layer, the lithosphere.

Key Terms
topography	landform	plateau
elevation	region	lithosphere
relief	plain	atmosphere
landform	mountain	hydrosphere
	mountain range	biosphere

SECTION 2 Mapping Earth's Surface

Key Ideas
◆ Maps and globes are drawn to scale to show features on Earth's surface as seen from above.
◆ The grid of latitude and longitude lines can be used to locate points on Earth's surface.

Key Terms
map	key	degree
globe	equator	latitude
scale	hemisphere	longitude
symbols	prime meridian	map projection

SECTION 3 Maps in the Computer Age

INTEGRATING TECHNOLOGY

Key Ideas
◆ Instruments carried aboard satellites in orbit around Earth make pictures of the surface called satellite images.
◆ Computers are used to store and display the information used in making maps.

Key Terms
satellite image   digitizing
pixel

SECTION 4 Topographic Maps

Key Ideas
◆ Topographic maps portray the elevation, relief, and slope of the landforms in an area.
◆ Contour lines are used on a topographic map to show elevation and relief.
◆ The contour interval of a topographic map is the amount that elevation increases or decreases between contour lines.
◆ In addition to showing elevation and relief, topographic maps include a variety of other natural and human-made features.

Key Terms
topographic map	contour interval
contour line	Global Positioning System

Organizing Information

Concept Map Copy the concept map about landforms onto a separate piece of paper. Then complete it and add a title. (For more on concept maps, see the Skills Handbook.)

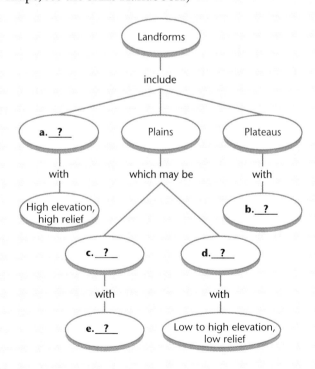

Reviewing Content

 For more review of key concepts, see the Interactive Student Tutorial CD-ROM.

Multiple Choice
Choose the letter of the best answer.

1. A landform that has high elevation but a mostly flat surface is a
   a. coastal plain.   b. mountain.
   c. mountain belt.   d. plateau.
2. Of the Earth's four "spheres," the one that extends into all the others is the
   a. lithosphere.   b. hydrosphere.
   c. biosphere.   d. atmosphere.
3. Latitude is a measurement of distance north or south of the
   a. hemispheres.   b. equator.
   c. axis.   d. prime meridian.
4. To show the continents without distorting their relative sizes and shapes, a mapmaker would choose a
   a. Mercator projection.
   b. globe.
   c. equal-area projection.
   d. topographic map.
5. On a topographic map, the contour lines form a V at a
   a. hilltop.   b. level area.
   c. depression.   d. valley.

True or False
If the statement is true, write true. If it is false, change the underlined word or words to make the statement true.

6. <u>Relief</u> measures a landform's height above sea level.
7. Going north or south from the <u>prime meridian</u>, the distance to one of the poles is 90 degrees.
8. Computers use data about Earth's surface that has been <u>digitized</u>, or put in the form of numbers.
9. If contour lines on a slope are spaced <u>wide apart</u>, then the slope is very steep.
10. Contour lines that form a closed loop marked with dashes indicate a <u>depression</u>.

Checking Concepts

11. What do geologists call an area where there is mostly one kind of topography?
12. What is a mountain range?
13. Compare the elevation of a coastal plain to that of an interior plain.
14. The South Island of New Zealand lies at about 170° E. What hemisphere is it in?
15. Could contour lines on a map ever cross? Explain.
16. Which would be more likely to show a shallow, 1.5-meter-deep depression in the ground: a 1-meter contour interval or a 5-meter contour interval? Explain.
17. **Writing to Learn** With your family, you make a car trip across the United States along the latitude line 35° N. Write a series of postcards to friends describing the landforms that you see on your trip. Use Appendix B to determine what the land is like along your route.

Thinking Critically

18. **Applying Concepts** Earth's diameter is about 13,000 kilometers. If a globe has a diameter of 0.5 meter, write the globe's scale as a ratio. What distance on Earth would 1 centimeter on the globe represent?
19. **Inferring** An airplane flies directly west at 1,000 kilometers per hour. Without changing direction, the plane returns to its starting point in just one hour. What can you infer about the plane's route with regard to lines of latitude and longitude? Explain.
20. **Observing** Using an atlas, find the latitude and longitude of San Francisco, California; Wichita, Kansas; and Richmond, Virginia. What do these three cities have in common?
21. **Comparing and Contrasting** How is mapmaking with computers different from earlier mapmaking techniques?
22. **Problem Solving** Your community has decided to build a zoo for animals from many regions of Earth. How could you use topographic maps of your area to help decide on the best location for the zoo?

Applying Skills

This map shows part of Acadia National Park in Maine. The contour interval is 20 feet. Use the map to answer Questions 23–25.

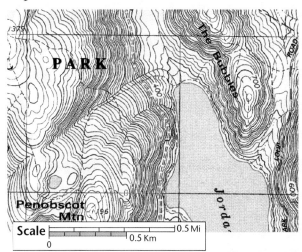

Scale 0.5 Mi / 0.5 Km / 0

23. Interpreting Maps

A. What is the elevation of the large lake?

B. Which of the two Bubbles is higher?

24. **Calculating** Use the map scale to calculate the distance from the top of Penobscot Mountain to the large lake.

25. **Inferring** How can you tell whether the streams flow into or out of the large lake?

Project Wrap Up Present your map to the class. Discuss the natural and physical features found on your site. What symbols did you use to represent these features? How did you measure and locate them on your map? How accurate is your map? Ask your classmates how you could improve your map.

Reflect and Record Write an evaluation of your map. What would you change about it? What would you keep the same? Does your map give others a clear idea of what the land looks like?

Test Preparation

Use these questions to prepare for standardized tests.

The map shows part of Earth's surface with a grid of latitude and longitude lines. Study the map. Then answer Questions 26–30.

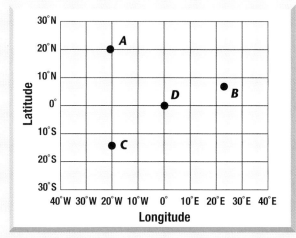

26. The horizontal line labeled 0° is called the
    a. horizon line.   **b.** equator.
    c. prime meridian.   **d.** contour line.

27. The latitude and longitude of point B is best given by
    a. 25°S 7°W.   **b.** 7°N 25°W.
    c. 7°E 25°N.   **d.** 7°N 25°E.

28. In which two hemispheres is point C located?
    a. western and southern hemispheres
    b. northern and eastern hemispheres
    c. eastern and western hemispheres
    d. western and northern hemispheres

29. The north-south distance in degrees from point A to Point C is about
    a. 15°.   **b.** 35°.
    c. 25°.   **d.** 0°.

30. Suppose you start at point D and travel southwest to point C. Through how many degrees of longitude have you traveled?
    a. 20°   **b.** 15°
    c. 60°   **d.** 30°

CHAPTER
2 Weathering and Soil Formation

WEB ACTIVITY
www.phschool.com

Integrating Environmental Science

2 Soils for Seeds

High above Paris, weathering attacks limestone statues that are hundreds of years old. The process of weathering affects all rocks exposed on Earth's surface. Weathering breaks rock down into smaller and smaller particles. When other ingredients, such as decayed plant and animal materials, mix with the rock particles, the mixture is called soil. In this chapter, you will test how soil and other growing materials affect the growth of plants.

Your Goal To determine how soil composition affects the growth of bean seeds.

To complete this project successfully, you must
◆ examine your different growing materials and compare their particle size, shape, and composition
◆ compare how bean seeds grow in several different growing materials
◆ determine what type of soil or growing material is best for young bean plants

Get Started With your group, brainstorm what types of soil and other growing materials you will use in your experiment. Also consider these questions: What are the different variables that affect the growth of plants? How will you control these variables in your experiment? How will you measure the growth of your bean plants? Plan your experiment and obtain your teacher's approval.

Check Your Progress You will be working on this project as you study this chapter. To keep your project on track, look for Check Your Progress boxes at the following points.
Section 2 Review, page 55: Describe the different growing materials you have collected, and plant your bean seeds.
Section 3 Review, page 60: Observe and record the results of the growth of bean plants.

Wrap Up At the end of the chapter (page 63), you will present your results to the class. Your presentation will analyze how well bean plants grew in the different types of growing materials.

These stone gargoyles on the Cathedral of Notre Dame in Paris, France, are wearing away because of weathering.

① Rocks and Weathering

How Fast Can It Fizz?

1. Place a fizzing antacid tablet in a small beaker. Then grind up a second tablet and place it in another beaker. The whole tablet is a model of solid rock. The ground-up tablet is a model of rock fragments.

2. Add 100 mL of warm water to the beaker containing the whole tablet. Then stir with a stirring rod until the tablet dissolves completely. Use a stopwatch to time how long it takes.

3. Add 100 mL of warm water to the beaker containing the ground-up tablet. Then stir until all of the ground-up tablet dissolves. Time how long it takes.

Think It Over

Inferring Which dissolved faster, the whole antacid tablet or the ground-up tablet? What difference between the two affected how long it took them to dissolve?

GUIDE FOR READING

◆ What causes mechanical weathering?

◆ What causes chemical weathering?

◆ What determines how fast weathering occurs?

Reading Tip As you read, use the headings to make an outline about weathering.

Imagine a hike that lasts for months and covers hundreds of kilometers. Each year, many hikers go on such treks. They hike trails that run the length of America's great mountain ranges. For example, the John Muir Trail follows the Sierra Nevada mountains. The Sierras extend about 640 kilometers along the eastern side of California. In the east, the Appalachian Trail follows the Appalachian Mountains. The Appalachians stretch more than 2,000 kilometers from Alabama to Maine.

The two trails cross very different landscapes. The Sierras are rocky and steep, with many peaks rising 3,000 meters above sea level. The Appalachians are more rounded and gently sloping, and are covered with soil and plants. The highest peaks in the Appalachians are less than half the elevation of the highest peaks in the Sierras. Which mountain range do you think is older? The Appalachians formed more than 250 million years ago. The Sierras formed only within the last 10 million years. The forces that wear down rock on Earth's surface have had much longer to grind down the Appalachians.

The Effects of Weathering

The process of mountain building thrusts rock up to the Earth's surface. There, the rock becomes exposed to weathering. **Weathering** is the process that breaks down rock and other substances at Earth's surface. Heat, cold, water, and ice all contribute to weathering. So do the oxygen and carbon dioxide in the atmosphere. Repeated freezing

and thawing, for example, can crack rock apart into smaller pieces. Rainwater can dissolve minerals that bind rock together. You don't need to go to the mountains to see examples of weathering. The forces that wear down mountains also cause bicycles to rust, paint to peel, sidewalks to crack, and potholes to form.

The forces of weathering break rocks into smaller and smaller pieces. Then the forces of erosion carry the pieces away. **Erosion** (ee ROH zhun) is the movement of rock particles by wind, water, ice, or gravity. Weathering and erosion work together continuously to wear down and carry away the rocks at Earth's surface.

There are two kinds of weathering: mechanical weathering and chemical weathering. Both types of weathering act slowly, but over time they break down even the biggest, hardest rocks.

☑ *Checkpoint* *What is the difference between weathering and erosion?*

Mechanical Weathering

If you hit a rock hard enough with a hammer, the rock will break into pieces. Some forces of weathering can also break rock into pieces. The type of weathering in which rock is physically broken into smaller pieces is called **mechanical weathering.** These smaller pieces of rock have the same composition as the rock they came from. If you have seen rocks that are cracked or peeling in layers, then you have seen rocks that are undergoing mechanical weathering.

Mechanical weathering breaks rock into pieces by freezing and thawing, release of pressure, growth of plants, actions of animals, and abrasion. The term **abrasion** (uh BRAY zhun) refers to the grinding away of rock by rock particles carried by water, ice, wind, or gravity. Mechanical weathering works slowly. But over very long periods of time, it does more than wear down rocks. Mechanical weathering eventually wears away whole mountains.

Figure 1 The jagged, rocky peaks of the Sierra Nevadas (left) show that the mountains are young. The more gently sloping Appalachians (right) have been exposed to weathering for 250 million years.

 **INTEGRATING PHYSICS** In cool climates, the most important force of mechanical weathering is freezing and thawing of water. Water seeps into cracks in rocks and then freezes when the temperature drops. Water expands when it freezes. Ice therefore acts like a wedge, a simple machine that forces things apart. Wedges of ice in rocks widen and deepen cracks. This process is called **ice wedging.** When the ice melts, the water seeps deeper into the cracks. With repeated freezing and thawing, the cracks slowly expand until pieces of rock break off. *Exploring the Forces of Mechanical Weathering* shows how this process weathers rock.

☑ *Checkpoint* How does ice wedging weather rock?

EXPLORING the Forces of Mechanical Weathering

Mechanical weathering affects all the rock on Earth's surface. Given enough time, mechanical weathering can break down a massive mountain into tiny particles of sand.

Release of Pressure
As erosion removes material from the surface of a mass of rock, pressure on the rock is reduced. This release of pressure causes the outside of the rock to crack and flake off like the layers of an onion.

Freezing and Thawing
When water freezes in a crack in a rock, it expands and makes the crack bigger. The process of ice wedging also widens cracks in sidewalks and causes potholes in streets.

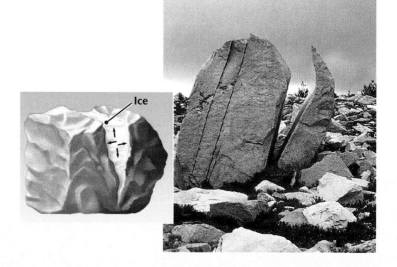

Chemical Weathering

In addition to mechanical weathering, another type of weathering attacks rock. **Chemical weathering** is the process that breaks down rock through chemical changes. **The agents of chemical weathering include water, oxygen, carbon dioxide, living organisms, and acid rain.**

Chemical weathering produces rock particles that have a different mineral makeup from the rock they came from. Each rock is made up of one or more minerals. For example, granite is made up of several minerals, including feldspar, quartz, and mica. But chemical weathering of granite eventually changes the feldspar minerals to clay minerals.

Plant Growth
Roots of trees and other plants enter cracks in rocks. As the roots grow, they force the cracks farther apart. Over time, the roots of even small plants can pry apart cracked rocks.

Abrasion
Sand and other rock particles that are carried by wind, water, or ice can wear away exposed rock surfaces like sandpaper on wood. Wind-driven sand helped shape the rocks shown here.

Animal Actions
Animals that burrow in the ground—including moles, gophers, prairie dogs, and some insects—loosen and break apart rocks in the soil.

Figure 2 As weathering breaks apart rock, the surface area exposed to further weathering increases.

Chemical weathering creates holes or soft spots in rock, so the rock breaks apart more easily. Chemical and mechanical weathering often work together. As mechanical weathering breaks rock into pieces, more surface area becomes exposed to chemical weathering. The Discover activity in this section shows how increasing the surface area increases the rate of a chemical reaction.

Water Water is the most important agent of chemical weathering. Water weathers rock by dissolving it. When a rock or other substance dissolves in water, it mixes uniformly throughout the water to make a solution. Over time, many rocks will dissolve in water.

Oxygen The oxygen gas in air is an important cause of chemical weathering. If you have ever left a bicycle or metal tool outside in the rain, then you have seen how oxygen can weather iron. Iron combines with oxygen in the presence of water in a process called oxidation. The product of oxidation is rust. Rock that contains iron also oxidizes, or rusts. Rust makes rock soft and crumbly and gives it a red or brown color.

Carbon Dioxide Another gas found in air, carbon dioxide, also causes chemical weathering. Carbon dioxide becomes dissolved in rainwater and in water that sinks through air pockets in the soil. The result is a weak acid called carbonic acid. Carbonic acid easily weathers marble and limestone.

Living Organisms Imagine a seed landing on a rock face. As it sprouts, its roots push into cracks in the rock. As the plant's roots grow, they produce weak acids that slowly dissolve rock around the roots. Lichens—plantlike organisms that grow on rocks—also produce weak acids that chemically weather rock.

Acid Rain Over the past 150 years, people have been burning

INTEGRATING large amounts of coal, oil, and gas
ENVIRONMENTAL SCIENCE for energy. Burning these fuels can pollute the air with sulfur, carbon, and nitrogen compounds. Such compounds react chemically with the water vapor in clouds, forming acids. These acids mix with raindrops and fall as acid rain. Acid rain causes very rapid chemical weathering.

Rate of Weathering

Visitors to New England's historic cemeteries may notice a surprising fact. Slate tombstones from the 1700s are less weathered and easier to read than marble gravestones from the 1800s. Why is this so? **The most important factors that determine the rate at which weathering occurs are type of rock and climate.**

Type of Rock Some kinds of rocks weather more rapidly than others. The minerals that make up the rock determine how fast it weathers. Rock made of minerals that do not dissolve easily in water weathers slowly. Rock made of minerals that dissolve easily in water weathers faster.

Some rock weathers easily because it is permeable. **Permeable** (PUR mee uh bul) means that a material is full of tiny, connected air spaces that allow water to seep through it. Permeable rock weathers chemically at a fast rate. Why? As water seeps through the spaces in the rock, it removes dissolved material formed by weathering.

Climate Climate refers to the average weather conditions in an area. Both chemical and mechanical weathering occur faster in wet climates. Rainfall provides the water needed for chemical changes as well as for freezing and thawing.

Chemical reactions occur faster at higher temperatures. That is why chemical weathering occurs more quickly where the climate is both hot and wet. Granite, for example, is a very hard rock that forms when molten material cools inside Earth. Granite weathers so slowly in cool climates that it is often used as a building stone. But in hot and wet climates, granite weathers faster and eventually crumbles apart.

Figure 3 The rate of weathering of these tombstones depends on the type of rock. Slate (top) resists weathering better than marble (bottom). *Inferring What type of weathering probably wore away the letters on the marble tombstone?*

Section 1 Review

1. What factors cause mechanical weathering?
2. Describe three causes of chemical weathering.
3. What factors affect the rate of weathering?
4. Explain why chemical weathering occurs faster in hot, wet climates than in cool, dry climates.
5. **Thinking Critically Predicting** Suppose you see a large boulder with several cracks in it. What would you expect to see if you could observe the boulder again in several hundred years? Explain.

Science at Home

Here's how to demonstrate one type of weathering for your family. Plug one end of a drinking straw with a small piece of clay. Fill the straw with water. Now plug the top of the straw with clay. Make sure that the clay plugs do not leak. Lay the straw flat in the freezer overnight. Remove the straw the next day. What happened to the clay plugs? What process produced this result? Be sure to dispose of the straw so that no one will use it for drinking.

ROCK SHAKE

Which do you think would weather faster, a rock attacked by plant acids or a rock in the rushing waters of a stream? Many factors affect the rate at which rock weathers. In this lab, you will compare the rates of weathering that take place under different conditions.

Problem

How will shaking and acid conditions affect the rate at which limestone weathers?

Materials

300 mL of water
balance
paper towels
masking tape
2 pieces of thin cloth
marking pen or pencil
300 mL of vinegar, an acid
plastic graduated cylinder, 250 mL
80 small pieces of water-soaked limestone
4 watertight plastic containers with
   screw-on caps, 500-mL

Procedure

Part 1— Day 1

1. Using masking tape, label the four 500-mL containers A, B, C, and D.
2. Separate the 80 pieces of limestone into four sets of 20.
3. Copy the data table in your notebook. Then place the first 20 pieces of limestone on the balance and record their mass in the data table. Place the rocks in Container A.
4. Repeat Step 3 for the other sets of rocks and place them in containers B, C, and D.
5. Pour 150 mL of water into container A and container B. Put caps on both containers.
6. Pour 150 mL of vinegar into container C and also into container D. Put caps on both containers.
7. Predict the effect of weathering on the mass of the limestone pieces. Which will weather more: the limestone in water or the limestone in vinegar? (*Hint:* Vinegar is an acid.) Also predict the effect of shaking on the limestone in containers B and D. Record your predictions in your notebook.
8. Allow the pieces to soak overnight.

Container	Total Mass Start	Total Mass Next Day	Change in Mass	Percent Change in Mass
A (water, no shaking)				
B (water, shaking)				
C (vinegar, no shaking)				
D (vinegar, shaking)				

Part 2—Day 2

9. Screw the caps tightly on containers B and D. Shake both containers for 10 to 15 minutes. Make sure that each container is shaken for exactly the same amount of time and at the same intensity. After shaking, set the containers aside. Do not shake containers A and C.

10. Open the top of container A. Place one piece of thin cloth over the opening of the container. Carefully pour all of the water out through the cloth into a waste container. Be careful not to let any of the pieces flow out with the water. Dry these pieces carefully and record their mass in your data table.

11. Next, determine how much limestone was lost through weathering in container A. (*Hint:* Subtract the mass of the limestone pieces remaining on Day 2 from the mass of the pieces on Day 1.)

12. Repeat Steps 10 and 11 for containers B, C, and D.

Analyze and Conclude

1. Calculate the percent change in mass of the 20 pieces for each container.

$$\% \text{ change} = \frac{\text{Change in mass} \times 100}{\text{Total mass start}}$$

Record the results in the data table.

2. Do your data show a change in mass of the 20 pieces in each of the four containers?

3. Is there a greater change in total mass for the pieces in one container than for the pieces in another? Explain.

4. How correct were your predictions of how shaking and acid would affect the weathering of limestone? Explain.

5. If your data showed a greater change in the mass of the pieces in one of the containers, how might this change be explained?

6. **Think About It** Based on your data, which variable do you think was more responsible for breaking down the limestone: the vinegar or the shaking? Explain.

Design an Experiment

Would your results for this experiment change if you changed the variables? For example, you could soak or shake the pieces for a longer time, or test rocks other than limestone. You could also test whether adding more limestone pieces (30 rather than 20 in each set) would make a difference in the outcome. Design an experiment on the rate of weathering to test the effects of changing one of these variables. Have your teacher approve your plan before you begin.

Preserving Stone Monuments

A statue with a human head and a lion's body crouches in the desert beside the pyramids of Egypt. This is the great Sphinx. It was carved out of limestone about 4,500 years ago. Thousands of years of weathering by water, wind, and sand have worn away much of the Sphinx's face. In the 1800s, sand that had protected the Sphinx's body was cleared away. Weathering attacked the newly exposed parts of the Sphinx. Flakes and even chunks of stone fell from the statue. Workers tried to repair the Sphinx with cement. But the repairs weakened the statue and changed its shape.

The Issues

Should Structures Be Restored?
Weathering threatens many ancient stone monuments throughout the world. Pollutants in air and rain make stone weather faster. But there are ways to slow the weathering of a monument without changing or damaging it. In 1998, workers in Egypt completed a new restoration of the Sphinx. They removed the added cement. They replaced the damaged stones with new, hand-cut limestone blocks of the same size and weight. The new stone will help protect what remains of the monument. Visitors to the Sphinx will now see only the original statue and repairs made with original materials. The new repairs preserve the statue's original shape.

Most people want the Sphinx and other monuments to be restored. But restoration is time-consuming and very expensive. And in some cases, repair work can damage or change the original structure.

Can New Technology Slow Weathering?
Advances in technology may provide some solutions. At the Sphinx, scientists measure wind direction, wind speed, and moisture in the air. This information helps scientists follow the weathering process and provides data that will help prevent more damage. Similar instruments are used at other monuments.

Other scientists are working on a way of coating stone with a chemical compound to strengthen and repair the surface. So far, they have found a compound that sticks well to sandstone, but not to marble or limestone.

What Else Can People Do? Repair and restoration are not the only options. Some say that ancient monuments should be buried again after being uncovered by archaeologists. Some people suggest that the Sphinx itself should be reburied in the sand that protected it for so many centuries. But scholars, archaeologists, and tourists disagree. Meanwhile, as people seek solutions, rain, wind, sun, and polluted air continue to take their toll.

You Decide

1. Identify the Problem
In your own words, explain the difficulties involved in preserving ancient monuments.

2. Analyze the Options
List methods for preserving ancient buildings and monuments. Note the advantages and disadvantages of repair work, technology, and other approaches.

3. Find a Solution
Make a plan to preserve a monument in your city. Write your recommendations in the form of a letter to a city mayor or town council.

SECTION 2 Soil Formation and Composition

DISCOVER ································ ACTIVITY

What Is Soil?

1. Use a toothpick to separate a sample of soil into individual particles. With a hand lens, try to identify the different types of particles in the sample. Wash your hands when you are finished.

2. Write a "recipe" for the sample of soil, naming each of the "ingredients" that you think the soil contains. Include what percentage of each ingredient would be needed to make up the soil.

3. Compare your recipe with those of your classmates.

Think It Over
Forming Operational Definitions Based on your observations, how would you define *soil*?

A bare rock surface does not look like a spot where a plant could grow. But look more closely. In that hard surface is a small crack. Over many years, mechanical and chemical weathering will slowly enlarge the crack. Rain and wind will bring bits of weathered rock, dust, and dry leaves. The wind also may carry tiny seeds. With enough moisture, a seed will sprout and take root. Then, when the plant blossoms a few months later, the rock itself will seem to have burst into flower.

Soil Formation

The crack in the rock seems to have little in common with a flower garden containing thick, rich soil. But soil is what the weathered rock and other materials in the crack have started to become. **Soil** is the loose, weathered material on Earth's surface in which plants can grow. **Soil forms as rock is broken down by weathering and mixes with other materials on the surface.**

Soil is constantly being formed wherever bedrock is exposed. **Bedrock** is the solid layer of rock beneath the soil. Once exposed at the surface, bedrock gradually weathers into smaller and smaller particles that are the basic material of soil.

GUIDE FOR READING

◆ How does soil form?

◆ What is soil made of?

◆ What is the role of plants and animals in soil formation?

Reading Tip Before you read, rewrite the headings as *how, what, where,* and *why* questions. Then look for answers as you read.

Figure 4 A crack between rocks holds just enough soil for this plant.

Composition of Loam

Silt 18%

Air 25%

Sand 18%

Water 25%

Clay 9%

Organic matter 5%

Figure 5 Loam, a type of soil, is made up of air, water, and organic matter as well as materials from weathered rock.
Interpreting Graphs What two materials make up the major portion of this soil?

Soil Composition

Soil is more than just particles of weathered bedrock. **Soil is a mixture of rock particles, minerals, decayed organic material, air, and water.**

The type of rock particles and minerals in any given soil depends on two factors: the bedrock that was weathered to form the soil and the type of weathering. Together, sand, silt, and clay make up the portion of soil that comes from weathered rock.

The decayed organic material in soil is humus. **Humus** (HYOO mus) is a dark-colored substance that forms as plant and animal remains decay. Humus helps create spaces in soil for the air and water that plants must have. Humus is also rich in the nitrogen, sulfur, phosphorus, and potassium that plants need to grow.

Soil Texture

Sand feels coarse and grainy, but clay feels smooth and silky. These differences are differences in texture. Soil texture depends on the size of individual soil particles.

The particles of rock in soil are classified by size. As you can see in Figure 6, the largest soil particles are gravel. Small pebbles and even large boulders are considered gravel. Next in size are particles of sand, followed by silt particles, which are smaller than sand. The smallest soil particles are clay. Clay particles are smaller than the period at the end of this sentence.

Soil texture is important for plant growth. Soil that is mostly clay has a dense, heavy texture. Some clay soils hold a lot of water, so plants grown in them may "drown" for lack of air. In contrast, sandy soil has a coarse texture. Water quickly drains through it, so plants may die for lack of water.

Soil that is made up of about equal parts of clay, sand, and silt is called **loam.** It has a crumbly texture that holds both air and water. Loam is best for growing most types of plants.

Figure 6 Soil particles range in size from gravel to clay particles too small to be seen by the unaided eye. The sand, silt, and clay shown here have been enlarged.

Gravel	Sand	Silt	Clay
2 mm and larger	less than 2 mm	less than $\frac{1}{16}$ mm	less than $\frac{1}{256}$ mm

Soil Horizons

Soil formation continues over a long period of time. Gradually, soil develops layers called horizons. A **soil horizon** is a layer of soil that differs in color and texture from the layers above or below it.

If you dug a hole in the ground about half a meter deep, you would see the different soil horizons. Figure 7 shows how soil scientists classify the soil into three horizons. The A horizon is made up of **topsoil,** a crumbly, dark brown soil that is a mixture of humus, clay, and other minerals. The B horizon, often called **subsoil,** usually consists of clay and other particles washed down from the A horizon, but little humus. The C horizon contains only partly weathered rock.

☑ *Checkpoint* What are soil horizons?

The Rate of Soil Formation

The rate at which soil forms depends on the climate and type of rock. Remember that weathering occurs most rapidly in areas with a warm, rainy climate. As a result, soil develops more quickly in these areas. In contrast, weathering and soil formation take place slowly in areas where the climate is cold and dry.

Some types of rock weather and form soil faster than others. For example, limestone weathers faster than granite. Thus, soil forms more quickly from limestone than from granite.

Sharpen your Skills

Predicting ACTIVITY

Gardeners often improve soil by adding materials to it. These added materials change the soil's composition. They make the soil more fertile or improve its ability to hold water. For example, a gardener might add compost (partly decayed leaves) to sandy soil. How would the compost change the sandy soil?

Figure 7 Soil horizons form in three steps.

1. The C horizon forms as bedrock weathers and rock breaks up into soil particles.

2. The A horizon develops from the C horizon when plant roots weather the rock mechanically and chemically. Plants also add organic material to the soil.

3. The B horizon develops as rainwater washes clay and minerals from the A horizon to the B horizon.

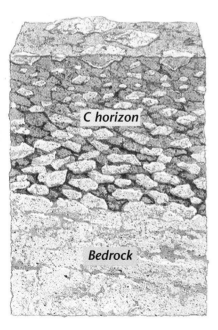

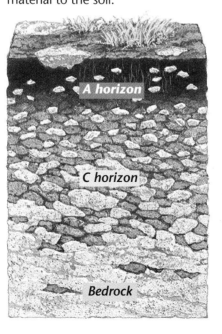

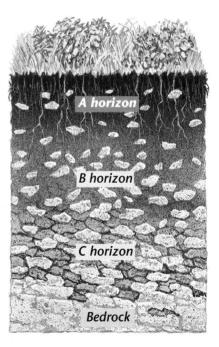

Life in Soil

INTEGRATING LIFE SCIENCE Soil is more than just bits of rock. If you look closely at some soil, you can see that it is teeming with living things. **Some soil organisms mix the soil and make spaces in it for air and water. Other soil organisms make humus, the material that makes soil fertile.** Fertile soil is rich in nutrients that plants need, such as nitrogen and phosphorus.

Plants contribute most of the organic remains that form humus. As plants shed leaves, they form a loose layer called **litter.**

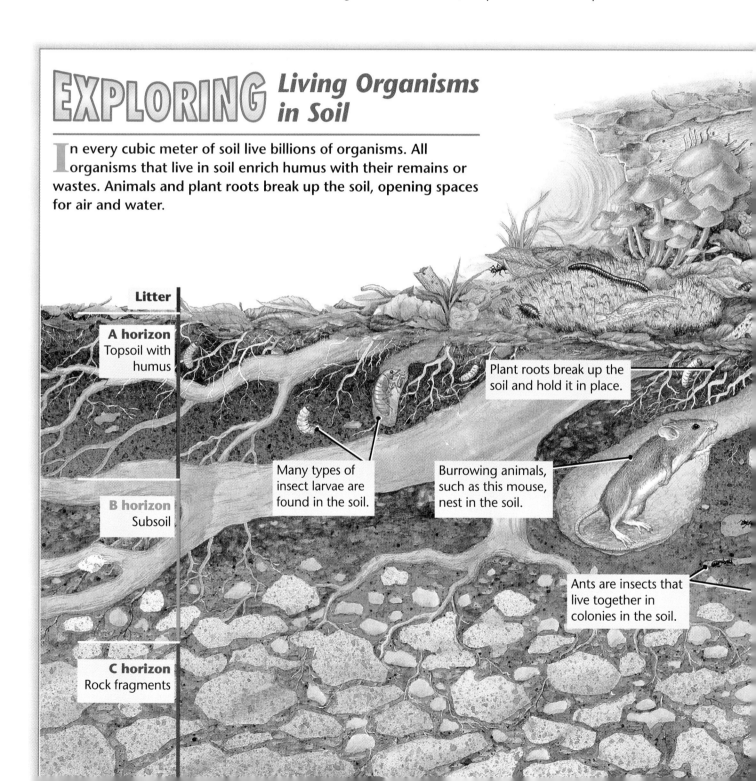

EXPLORING *Living Organisms in Soil*

In every cubic meter of soil live billions of organisms. All organisms that live in soil enrich humus with their remains or wastes. Animals and plant roots break up the soil, opening spaces for air and water.

Litter

A horizon
Topsoil with humus

B horizon
Subsoil

C horizon
Rock fragments

Plant roots break up the soil and hold it in place.

Many types of insect larvae are found in the soil.

Burrowing animals, such as this mouse, nest in the soil.

Ants are insects that live together in colonies in the soil.

When plants die, their remains fall to the ground and become part of the litter. Plant roots also die and begin to decay underground. Although plant remains are full of stored nutrients, they are not yet humus.

Humus forms in a process called decomposition. As decomposition occurs, organisms that live in soil turn dead organic material into humus. These organisms are called decomposers. **Decomposers** are the organisms that break the remains of dead organisms into smaller pieces and digest them with chemicals.

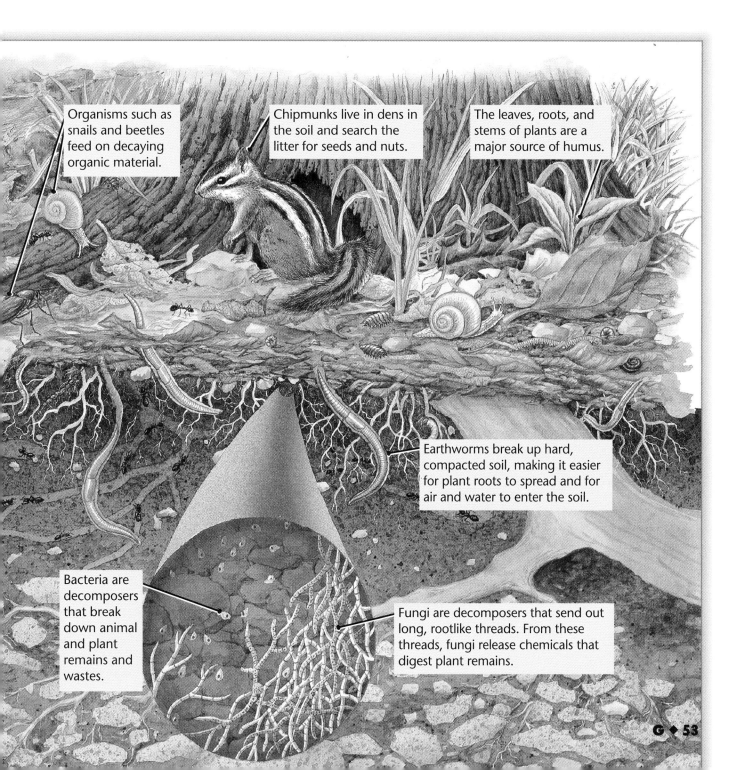

Organisms such as snails and beetles feed on decaying organic material.

Chipmunks live in dens in the soil and search the litter for seeds and nuts.

The leaves, roots, and stems of plants are a major source of humus.

Earthworms break up hard, compacted soil, making it easier for plant roots to spread and for air and water to enter the soil.

Bacteria are decomposers that break down animal and plant remains and wastes.

Fungi are decomposers that send out long, rootlike threads. From these threads, fungi release chemicals that digest plant remains.

A Square Meter of Soil

1. Outdoors, **ACTIVITY** measure an area of one square meter. Mark your square with string.

2. Observe the color and texture of the surface soil. Is it dry or moist? Does it contain sand, clay, or gravel? Are there plants, animals, or humus?

3. Use a trowel to dig down several centimeters into the soil. What is the soil's color and texture there?

4. When you finish, leave the soil as you found it. Wash your hands.

Drawing Conclusions What can you conclude about the soil's fertility? What evidence supports your conclusions?

Fungi, protists, bacteria, and worms are the main soil decomposers. Fungi are organisms such as molds and mushrooms. Fungi grow on, and digest, plant remains. Bacteria are microscopic decomposers that cause decay. Bacteria attack dead organisms and their wastes in soil. Other very small animals, such as mites and worms, also decompose dead organic material and mix it with the soil.

Earthworms do most of the work of mixing humus with other materials in soil. As earthworms eat their way through the soil, they carry humus down to the subsoil and subsoil up to the surface. Earthworms also pass out the soil they eat as waste. The waste soil is enriched with substances that plants need to grow, such as nitrogen.

Many burrowing mammals such as mice, moles, prairie dogs, and gophers break up hard, compacted soil and mix humus through it. These animals also add nitrogen to the soil when they excrete waste. They add organic material when they die and decay.

Earthworms and burrowing animals also help to aerate, or mix air into, the soil. Plant roots need the oxygen that this process adds to the soil.

☑ *Checkpoint* How do decomposers contribute to the formation of soil?

Soil Types in the United States

If you were traveling across the hills of north-central Georgia, you would see soils that seem to be made of red clay. In other parts of the country, soils can be black, brown, yellow, or gray. In the United States alone, differences in climate and local bedrock have led to the formation of thousands of different types of soil.

Figure 8 Earthworms break up the soil, allowing in air and water. An earthworm eats its own weight in soil every day.

Soils of North America

	Tundra soils	Form where it is cold year-round; thin soil with little humus.
	Northern forest soils	Form in cool, wet climates; range from thick and fertile to thin with little humus.
	Prairie soils	Form in cool, dry climates of grasslands; topsoil thick and rich in humus.
	Mountain soils	Topsoil often thin because cold temperatures slow chemical weathering and erosion causes soil loss.
	Southern forest soils	Form in warm, wet climates; may be low in humus.
	Desert soils	Form in dry areas with few plants and little chemical weathering; often sandy, thin soil that is low in humus.
	Tropical soils	Form in wet, tropical climates; often low in humus and minerals.

Scientists classify the different types of soil into groups. These groups are based partly on the climate in a region. The most common plants found in a region are also used to help classify the soil. In addition, scientists classify soil by its composition—whether it is rocky, sandy, or rich in clay. Major soil types found in North America include forest, prairie, desert, mountain, tundra, and tropical soils. Look at Figure 9 to see where each of the major soil types is found. Which soil type is found in your part of the country?

Figure 9 An area's climate and plant life help to determine what type of soil forms from bedrock. *Interpreting Maps Recall that soil forms more rapidly in warm, wet areas than in cold, dry areas. Which types of soil on the map would you expect to form most slowly?*

Section 2 Review

1. What role does weathering play in the formation of soil?
2. What are the different materials that make up soil?
3. How do plants and animals affect the formation and composition of soil?
4. How do forest soils differ from prairie soils?
5. **Thinking Critically Relating Cause and Effect** Earthworms breathe by absorbing air in the soil through their skin. Why do you think earthworms crawl to the surface when it rains? Explain.

Check Your Progress

CHAPTER PROJECT 2

Obtain samples of the soil and growing materials you will use to grow your bean seeds. Choices include sand, vermiculite, gravel, potting soil, and local topsoil. **CAUTION:** *Avoid collecting soil near animal droppings. Wash your hands after handling the soil.* Make notes describing each sample. Predict which soil or mixture will be best for the growth of bean seeds. Design a method for recording the growth of your bean plants. Plant the bean seeds in the growing materials.

Getting to Know the Soil

Soil scientists observe soil to determine its composition and how well it holds water. Farmers use this information in growing their crops.

Problem

What are the characteristics of a sample of soil?

Skills Focus

observing, inferring, posing questions

Materials

20–30 grams of soil
plastic spoon
plastic dropper
toothpick
water
stereomicroscope
graph paper ruled
    with 1- or 2-mm
    spacing
plastic petri dish or jar lid

Procedure

1. Your teacher will give you a dry sample of soil. As you observe the sample, record your observations in your lab notebook.
2. Spread half of the sample on the graph paper. Spread the soil thinly so that you can see the lines on the paper through the soil. Using the graph paper as a background, estimate the sizes of the particles that make up the soil.
3. Place the rest of the sample in the palm of your hand, rub it between your fingers, and squeeze it. Is it soft or gritty? Does it clump together or crumble when you squeeze it?

4. Place about half the sample in a plastic petri dish. Using the dropper, add water one drop at a time. Watch how the sample changes. Does any material in the sample float? As the sample gets wet, do you notice any odor?
5. Look at some of the soil under the stereomicroscope. (*Hint:* Use the toothpick to examine the particles in the soil.) Sketch what you see. Label the particles, such as gravel, organic matter, or strangely shaped grains.
6. Clean up and dispose of your soil sample as directed by your teacher. **CAUTION:** *Wash your hands when you finish handling the soil.*

Analyze and Conclude

1. What did you notice about the appearance of the soil sample when you first obtained it?
2. What can you infer about the composition of the soil from the different sizes of its particles? From your observations of its texture? From how the sample changed when water was added? What surprised you the most about the composition of your sample?
3. Based on the composition of your soil sample, can you determine the type of environment from which it was taken?
4. **Apply** List several questions that a soil scientist would need to answer to determine whether a soil sample was good for growing flowers or vegetables. Did your observations answer these questions for your soil sample?

More to Explore

Repeat the procedure using a soil sample from a different location. How does it compare with the first soil sample you tested?

SECTION 3 Soil Conservation

DISCOVER •••ACTIVITY••••

How Can You Keep Soil From Washing Away?

1. Pour about 500 mL of soil into a pie plate, forming a pile.

2. Devise a way to keep the soil from washing away when water is poured over it. To protect the pile of soil, you may use craft sticks, paper clips, pebbles, modeling clay, strips of paper, or other materials approved by your teacher.

3. After arranging your materials to protect the soil, hold a container containing 200 mL of water about 20 cm above the center of the soil. Slowly pour the water in a stream onto the pile of soil.

4. Compare your pan of soil with those of your classmates.

Think It Over

Observing Based on your observations, what do you think is the best way to prevent soil on a slope from washing away?

Suppose you were a settler traveling west in the early 1800s. Much of your journey would have been through vast, open grasslands called prairies. After the forests and mountains of the East, the prairies were an amazing sight. Grass taller than a person rippled and flowed in the wind like a sea of green.

The prairie soil was very fertile. It was rich with humus because of the tall grass. The **sod**—the thick mass of tough roots at the surface of the soil—kept the soil in place and held onto moisture.

The prairies covered a vast area. They included the eastern parts of Kansas, Nebraska, North and South Dakota, as well as Iowa and Illinois. Today, farms growing crops such as corn, soybeans, and wheat have replaced the prairies. But the prairie soils are still among the most fertile in the world.

GUIDE FOR READING

◆ Why is soil one of Earth's most valuable resources?

◆ What caused the Dust Bowl?

◆ What are some ways that soil can be conserved?

Reading Tip As you read, make a list of human activities that can harm the soil and a list of activities that can help save the soil.

The Value of Soil

Soil is one of Earth's most valuable resources because everything that lives on land depends directly or indirectly on soil. Plants depend directly on the soil to live and grow. Animals depend on plants—or on other animals that depend on plants—for food. Soil is a renewable resource that can be found wherever weathering occurs. But soil formation takes a long time. It can take hundreds of years for just a few centimeters of soil to form. The thick, fertile soil of the prairies took many thousands of years to develop.

Prairie grasses and wildflowers ▶

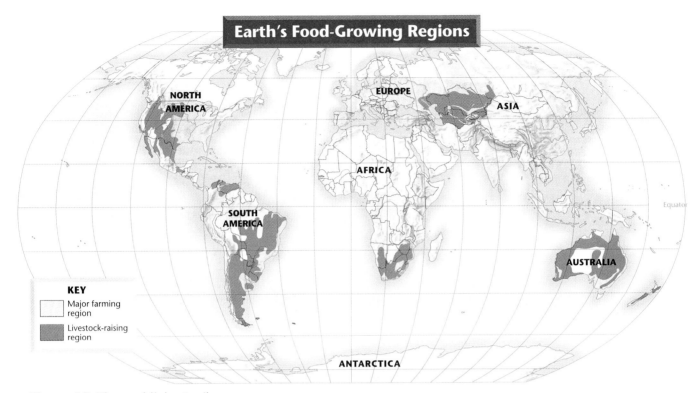

Earth's Food-Growing Regions

KEY
- Major farming region
- Livestock-raising region

Figure 10 The world's best soils for farming often are found in river valleys or interior and coastal plains. Areas too dry, too mountainous, or not fertile enough for farming may be used for grazing cattle, sheep, or other livestock.

Fertile soil is valuable because there is a limited supply. Less than one eighth of the land on Earth has soils that are well suited for farming. Figure 10 shows where these regions are located. In many areas, farming is difficult and little food is produced. The reasons for this include low soil fertility, lack of water, steep slopes, or a short growing season.

✓ *Checkpoint* Why is soil valuable?

Soil Damage and Loss

Soil is one of Earth's most important resources. But soil can be lost or damaged. For example, soil can become exhausted, or lose its fertility. This occurred in large parts of the South in the late 1800s. Soils in which only cotton had been grown were exhausted. Many farmers abandoned their farms. Early in the 1900s in Alabama, a scientist named George Washington Carver developed new crops and farming methods that helped to restore soil fertility in the South. Peanuts were one crop that helped make the soil fertile again.

Soil can be lost to erosion by water and wind. Water erosion can occur wherever soil is not protected by plant cover. Plants break the force of falling rain, and plant roots hold the soil together. Wind erosion is another cause of soil loss. Wind erosion, combined with farming methods that were not suited to dry conditions, caused the Dust Bowl on the Great Plains.

Figure 11 George Washington Carver (1864–1943) taught new methods of soil conservation to farmers in the South.

The Dust Bowl

Toward the end of the 1800s, farmers had settled most of the prairies. New settlers moved on to the Great Plains farther west. This region sweeps eastward from the base of the Rocky Mountains across the western parts of North and South Dakota, Nebraska, Kansas, Oklahoma, and Texas.

The soil of the Great Plains is fertile. But there is an important difference between the Great Plains and the prairie. Rainfall decreases steadily from east to west across the Great Plains. The tall grass gives way to shorter, thinner grass needing less moisture. **Plowing removed the grass from the Great Plains and exposed the soil. In times of drought, the topsoil quickly dried out, turned to dust, and blew away.**

By 1930, almost all of the Great Plains had been turned into farms or ranches. Then, several very dry years in a row turned the soil on parts of the Great Plains to dust. The wind blew the soil east in great, black clouds. The clouds turned the sky dark as far away as Chicago and even New York City. Eventually the soil blew out over the Atlantic Ocean, where it was lost forever.

The problem was most serious in the southern Plains states. There, the drought and topsoil loss lasted until 1938. This area, shown in Figure 12, was called the **Dust Bowl.** Many people in the Dust Bowl states abandoned their farms and moved away.

Language Arts CONNECTION

Woody Guthrie wrote and sang folk songs. Guthrie lived in Oklahoma and Texas at the time of the Dust Bowl and wrote a series of songs called "Dust Bowl Ballads." (A ballad is a song that tells a story.) One of the ballads describes how

We saw outside our window
Where wheat fields they had
* grown*
Was now a rippling ocean
Of dust the wind had blown.

In Your Journal

Write the words for a ballad that tells the story of a problem in your community and how you think the problem should be solved.

Figure 12 The Dust Bowl included western Oklahoma and parts of the surrounding states. Wind blew dry particles of soil into great clouds of dust that traveled thousands of kilometers.

Soil Conservation

The Dust Bowl helped people appreciate the value of soil. In the 1930s, with government support, farmers in the Great Plains and throughout the country began to take better care of their land. They adopted methods of farming that helped save the soil. Some of the methods were new. Others had been practiced for hundreds of years.

Farmers in the United States adopted modern methods of soil conservation. **Soil conservation** is the management of soil to prevent its destruction. **Two ways that soil can be conserved include contour plowing and conservation plowing.**

Contour plowing is the practice of plowing fields along the curves of a slope. This helps slow the runoff of excess rainfall and prevents it from washing the soil away.

Conservation plowing disturbs the soil and its plant cover as little as possible. Dead weeds and stalks of the previous year's crop are left in the ground to help return soil nutrients, retain moisture, and hold soil in place. This method is also called low-till or no-till plowing.

In grasslands such as the Great Plains, grazing livestock is an important use of the land. But if too many cattle graze on the grass during dry periods, the grass cover protecting the soil may be damaged. This exposes the soil to both wind and water erosion. To prevent damage to the soil, ranchers must limit the size of their herds.

Figure 13 Contour plowing (above) and conservation plowing (below) help prevent soil erosion. *Predicting How might conservation plowing affect the amount of humus in the soil?*

Section 3 Review

1. Explain the importance of soil as one of Earth's resources.
2. How did settlers on the Great Plains help create the Dust Bowl?
3. What are some techniques that farmers use to conserve soil?
4. **Thinking Critically Problem Solving** If you had to plant corn on a steep hillside, how would you do it so that rain would not wash the soil away?

Check Your Progress

CHAPTER PROJECT 2

Check your bean seeds daily and water them as needed. Count and record the number of seeds that sprout. You can also measure the height of each plant, count the number of leaves, and note the leaf color. After about 14 days, you should be able to make comparisons. What differences did you observe in the bean plants grown in the different materials? When did these differences appear? Based on your data, what conclusions can you draw about which material is best for growing bean plants?

SECTION 1 ## Rocks and Weathering

Key Ideas

◆ Rock weathers, or wears down, when it is exposed to air, water, weather, and living things at Earth's surface.

◆ Mechanical weathering breaks rock into smaller pieces. The agents of mechanical weathering include freezing and thawing, release of pressure, growth of plants, actions of animals, and abrasion.

◆ Chemical weathering changes the mineral content of rock. The agents of chemical weathering are water, oxygen, carbon dioxide, living organisms, and acid rain.

◆ Climate and rock type determine how fast weathering occurs.

Key Terms

weathering	ice wedging
erosion	chemical weathering
mechanical weathering	permeable
abrasion	

 SECTION 2 ## Soil Formation and Composition

Key Ideas

◆ Soil is made of small particles of rock mixed with the decaying remains of organisms.

◆ Soil forms in layers called horizons as bedrock weathers and organic materials build up.

◆ The three soil horizons are the A horizon, the B horizon, and the C horizon. The A horizon is made up of topsoil, which is rich in humus. The B horizon consists of clay and other particles washed down from the A horizon, but little humus. The C horizon is made up of partly weathered rock without clay or humus.

◆ Plants and animals break up and mix the soil, and also add the organic materials that form humus.

Key Terms

soil	loam	subsoil
bedrock	soil horizon	litter
humus	topsoil	decomposers

SECTION 3 ## Soil Conservation

INTEGRATING ENVIRONMENTAL SCIENCE

Key Ideas

◆ Soil is a valuable resource because life on land depends on it, yet it forms very slowly.

◆ Soil can be eroded away and its fertility can be decreased by improper farming practices.

◆ Soil can be conserved and its fertility can be maintained by using various methods of soil conservation.

Key Terms

sod	contour plowing
Dust Bowl	conservation plowing
soil conservation	

Organizing Information

Concept Map Copy the concept map about soil horizons onto a piece of paper. Then complete it and add a title. (For more on concept maps, see the Skills Handbook.)

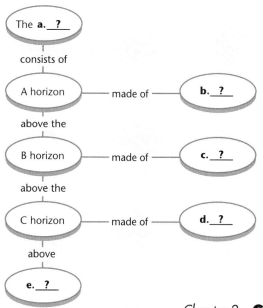

Reviewing Content

 For more review of key concepts, see the Interactive Student Tutorial CD-ROM.

Multiple Choice

Choose the letter of the best answer.

1. The most important force of mechanical weathering in cool climates is
   a. oxidation.
   b. freezing and thawing.
   c. animal activity.
   d. abrasion.
2. Most chemical weathering is caused by
   a. acid rain.
   b. water.
   c. oxygen.
   d. carbon dioxide.
3. The B horizon consists of
   a. subsoil.
   b. topsoil.
   c. rock particles.
   d. bedrock.
4. One of the best types of soil for farming is
   a. forest soil.
   b. mountain soil.
   c. tropical soil.
   d. prairie soil.
5. Most of the work of mixing humus into the soil is done by
   a. fungi.
   b. bacteria.
   c. earthworms.
   d. mites.

True or False

If the statement is true, write true. If it is false, change the underlined word or words to make the statement true.

6. <u>Mechanical weathering</u> is the movement of rock particles by wind, water, or ice.
7. Weathering occurs faster in a <u>wet</u> climate.
8. The decayed organic material in soil is called <u>loam</u>.
9. <u>Fungi</u> produce chemicals that digest plant remains.
10. Scientists classify types of soil based partly on a region's <u>climate</u>.

Checking Concepts

11. Where is mechanical weathering likely to occur more quickly: where the winter temperature usually stays below freezing, or where it more often shifts back and forth around the freezing point? Explain.
12. Briefly describe how soil is formed.
13. Which contains more humus, topsoil or subsoil?
14. Explain how plants can act as agents of both mechanical and chemical weathering.
15. What role did grass play in conserving the soil of the prairies?
16. How does conservation plowing contribute to soil conservation?
17. **Writing to Learn** Write a description of your life as an earthworm. What would it be like to live in the soil? What would you see? What would you eat? How would you move through the soil? How would you change it?

Thinking Critically

18. **Predicting** Suppose mechanical weathering breaks a rock into pieces. How would this affect the rate at which the rock weathers chemically?
19. **Classifying** Classify the following examples as either mechanical weathering or chemical weathering:
    A. Cracks appear in a sidewalk next to a large tree.
    B. A piece of limestone develops holes like Swiss cheese.
    C. A rock exposed at the surface slowly turns reddish brown.
20. **Developing Hypotheses** On the moon there is no air or water. Develop a hypothesis about how fast rocks would weather on the moon compared with their rate of weathering on Earth. Explain.
21. **Relating Cause and Effect** Two rocks, each in a different location, have been weathering for the same amount of time. Mature soil has formed from one rock but only immature soil from the other. What factors might have caused this difference in rate of soil formation?

Applying Skills

Use the following information to answer Questions 22–24. You have two samples of soil. One is mostly sand and one is mostly clay.

22. **Developing Hypotheses** Which soil sample do you think would lose water more quickly? Why?

23. **Designing Experiments** Design an experiment to test how quickly water passes through each soil sample.

24. **Posing Questions** Suppose you are a farmer who wants to grow soybeans in one of these two soils. What questions would you need to answer before choosing where to plant your soybeans?

Performance CHAPTER PROJECT **2** **Assessment**

Project Wrap Up You are ready to present your conclusions about what type of material is best for growing bean plants. Decide how to display the data you collected on the different materials. How did your group's results compare with those of the other groups in your class?

Reflect and Record In your journal, describe how well the results of your experiment matched your predictions. What have you learned from this project about soil characteristics that help plants to grow? What improvements could you make to your experiment?

Test Preparation

Use these questions to prepare for standardized tests.

Use the diagram of soil horizons to answer Questions 25–29.

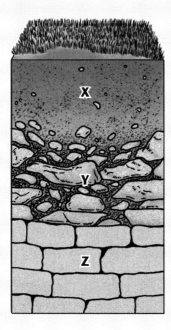

25. Layer X in the diagram consists of a mixture of humus, clay, and other minerals called
    a. litter. **b.** gravel.
    c. subsoil. **d.** topsoil.

26. Layer Y is made up of partly weathered rock called the
    a. C horizon.
    b. B horizon.
    c. A horizon.
    d. humus horizon.

27. One soil horizon, made up of clay and other particles but little humus, has not yet developed in this soil. The missing soil horizon is the
    a. A horizon.
    b. B horizon.
    c. C horizon.
    d. bedrock horizon.

28. The missing soil horizon will develop
    a. above layer X.
    b. below layer Z.
    c. between layers X and Y.
    d. between layers Y and Z.

29. In which layer or layers would you expect to find the most plant roots, insects, and other soil organisms?
    a. layers Y and Z **b.** layer Z
    c. layer Y **d.** layer X

CHAPTER

3 Erosion and Deposition

WEB ACTIVITY www.phschool.com

Changes In the Land

The view from the South Rim of the Grand Canyon in Arizona is one of Earth's most memorable sights.

The walls of the Grand Canyon reveal the colorful rock layers that make up the Colorado Plateau. What force shaped such a vast canyon? For about 6 million years the Colorado River has been cutting and grinding through the plateau. The river also carries away the broken particles of rock.

In this chapter you will explore the forces that change Earth's surface. Flowing water, frozen glaciers, waves, and wind all wear down and build up landforms. Throughout the chapter, you will build models showing how erosion shapes a landscape.

Your Goal To make three-dimensional models that show how the forces of erosion and deposition can change a landscape over millions of years.

To complete this project, you must
- ◆ make a three-dimensional model of a landscape
- ◆ predict how the model would be affected by erosion
- ◆ construct a second model showing how your landscape might look after erosion has continued for millions of years

Get Started Begin now by sketching a mountainous or hilly landscape. Include sharp peaks, deep valleys, a river or stream, and a coastline.

Check Your Progress You will be working on this project as you study this chapter. To keep your project on track, look for Check Your Progress boxes at the following points.
Section 3 Review, page 88: Draw and make your first model.
Section 4 Review, page 93: Begin to make your second model, showing how water and glaciers cause erosion.
Section 5 Review, page 97: Add the effects of wave erosion to the model.

Wrap Up At the end of the chapter (page 103), you will present your models to the class. In your presentation, you will explain how the landscape changed and predict how it might change in the future.

SECTION

① Changing Earth's Surface

DISCOVER ・・・・・・・・・・・・・・・・・・・・・・・・・・・・・・・・・・・・・**ACTIVITY**

How Does Gravity Affect Materials on a Slope?

1. Place a small board flat on your desk. Place a marble on the board and slowly tip the board up slightly at one end. Observe what happens.

2. Place a block of wood on the board. Slowly lift one end of the board and observe the result.

3. Next, cover the board and the wood block with sandpaper and repeat Step 2.

Think It Over

Developing Hypotheses How do the results of each step compare? Develop a hypothesis to explain the differences in your observations.

GUIDE FOR READING

◆ What processes wear down and build up Earth's surface?

◆ What force pulls rock and soil down slopes?

◆ What are the different types of mass movement?

Reading Tip As you read, make a list of main ideas and supporting details about erosion, deposition, and mass movement.

Madison River Canyon is a quiet wilderness area in the Rocky Mountains of Montana. In 1959, something happened to change the canyon forever. When a strong earthquake jolted nearby Yellowstone National Park, a mountainside along the canyon gave way. In a few seconds, nearly 30 million cubic meters of rock, soil, and trees slid into the canyon. If this much material were in the shape of a cube, then each side of the cube would be three times longer than a football field. Rock and soil from the landslide dammed the Madison River, forming a new lake.

Figure 1 During a landslide, loose rock and soil on the side of a mountain suddenly slide away from underlying bedrock. This landslide in Madison River Canyon, Montana, buried a highway and campground.

Wearing Down and Building Up

A landslide like the one in Madison River Canyon is a spectacular example of erosion. **Erosion** is the process by which natural forces move weathered rock and soil from one place to another. A landslide is a very rapid type of erosion. Other types of erosion move soil and rock more slowly. Gravity, running water, glaciers, waves, and wind can all cause erosion. You may have seen water carrying soil and gravel down a driveway after it rains. That's an example of erosion. Erosion also caused the damage to the road in Figure 2.

The material moved by erosion is **sediment.** Both weathering and erosion produce sediment. **Deposition** occurs where the agents of erosion lay down sediment. Deposition changes the shape of the land. You may have watched a playing child who picked up several toys and then carried them across a room and put them down. This child was acting something like an agent of erosion and deposition.

Weathering, erosion, and deposition act together in a cycle that wears down and builds up Earth's surface. Erosion and deposition are at work everywhere on Earth. Sometimes they work slowly. At other times, they work more quickly, such as during a thunderstorm. Then, heavy rain soaks into rock and soil. These water-soaked materials may then come loose suddenly and slide down a mountain. But as a mountain wears down in one place, new landforms build up in other places. Erosion and deposition are never-ending.

✓ *Checkpoint* *What happens to sediment as a result of erosion and deposition?*

Figure 2 Heavy winter rains washed out this California highway. *Relating Cause and Effect What caused the erosion that you can see in the photograph?*

Mass Movement

Imagine that you are sitting on a bicycle at the top of a hill. With only a slight push, you can coast down the hill. If the slope of the hill is very steep, you will reach a high speed before reaching the bottom. The force that pulls you and your bicycle downward is gravity. Gravity pulls everything toward the center of Earth.

Gravity is the force that moves rock and other materials downhill. Gravity causes **mass movement,** any one of several processes that move sediment downhill. Mass movement can be rapid or slow. **The different types of mass movement include landslides, mudslides, slump, and creep.**

Landslides The most destructive kind of mass movement is a landslide, which occurs when rock and soil slide quickly down a steep slope. Some landslides may contain huge masses of rock. But many landslides contain only a small amount of rock and soil. Such mass movement is common where road builders have cut highways through hills or mountains.

Figure 3 A mudflow caused by heavy rains raced through the streets of this town in Italy. *Relating Cause and Effect* What characteristic of soil can contribute to a mudflow?

Mudflows A mudflow is the rapid downhill movement of a mixture of water, rock, and soil. The amount of water in a mudflow can be as high as 60 percent. Mudflows often occur after heavy rains in a normally dry area. In clay soils with a high water content, mudflows may occur even on very gentle slopes. Under certain conditions, clay soils suddenly turn to liquid and begin to flow. For example, an earthquake can trigger both mudflows and landslides. Mudflows like the one in Figure 3 can be very dangerous.

Slump If you slump your shoulders, the entire upper part of your body drops down. In the type of mass movement known as slump, a mass of rock and soil suddenly slips down a slope. Unlike a landslide, the material in slump moves down in one large mass. It looks as if someone pulled the bottom out from under part of the slope. Figure 4 shows an example of slump. Slump often occurs when water soaks the base of a mass of soil that is rich in clay.

Figure 4 Slump can look as if a giant spoon has started to scoop a mass of soil out from a hillside.

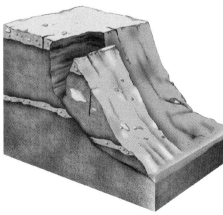

Creep Landscapes affected by creep may have the eerie, out-of-kilter look of a funhouse in an amusement park. Creep is the very slow downhill movement of rock and soil. It can even occur on gentle slopes. Like the movement of an hour hand on a clock, creep is so slow you can barely notice it. But you can see the effects of creep in objects such as telephone poles, gravestones, and fenceposts. Creep may tilt these objects at spooky angles. Creep often results from the freezing and thawing of water in cracked layers of rock beneath the soil. How have the trees in Figure 5 been affected by creep?

Sharpen your Skills

Observing ACTIVITY

Compare the examples of mass movement in Figures 4 and 5. Based on your observations, construct a table comparing slump and creep. Include the Earth materials involved, the type of slope, and the speed for each type of mass movement.

Figure 5 Creep has slowly tilted these trees downhill, causing their trunks to grow in a curve. *Predicting* If creep continues, how might it affect the road, the fence, and the electric power lines?

Section 1 Review   Science at Home

1. Explain the difference between erosion and deposition.
2. What force causes erosion?
3. What are four types of mass movement?
4. **Thinking Critically Relating Cause and Effect** Why would a landslide be more likely on a steep mountain than on a gently sloping hill?

After a rainstorm, take a walk with an adult family member around your neighborhood. Look for evidence of erosion. Try to find areas where there is loose soil, sand, gravel, or rock. (**CAUTION**: *Stay away from any large pile of loose sand or soil—it may slide without warning.*) Which areas have the most erosion? The least erosion? How does the slope of the ground affect the amount of erosion? Sketch or take photographs of the areas showing evidence of erosion.

Sand Hills

In this lab, you will develop and test a hypothesis about how mass movement affects the size and shape of a sand hill.

Problem

What is the relationship between the height and width of a sand hill?

Materials

Dry sand, 500 mL
Cardboard tube
Tray (about 15 cm × 45 cm × 60 cm)
Wooden barbecue skewer   Masking tape
Spoon   Ruler   Pencil or crayon
Several sheets of white paper

Procedure

1. Begin by observing how gravity causes mass movement in sand. To start, place the cardboard tube vertically in the center of the tray.
2. Using the spoon, fill the cardboard tube with the dry sand. Take care not to spill the sand around the outside of the tube.

3. Carefully lift the sand-filled tube straight up so that all the sand flows out. As you lift the tube, observe the sand's movement.
4. Develop a hypothesis explaining how you think the width of the sand pile is related to its height for different amounts of sand.
5. Empty the sand in the tray back into a container. Then set up your system for measuring the sand hill.
6. Copy the data table into your lab notebook.
7. Following Steps 1 through 3, make a new sand hill.

How to Measure a Sand Hill

1. Cover the bottom of the tray with unlined white paper and tape it firmly in place.
2. Mark off points 0.5 cm apart along one side of the paper in the tray.
3. Carefully draw the sand hill's outline on the paper. The line should go completely around the base of the hill.

4. Now measure the width of the hill against the marks you made along the edge of the paper.
5. Measure the sand hill's height by inserting a barbecue skewer through its center. Make a mark on the skewer at the top of the hill.
6. Remove the skewer and use the ruler to measure how much of the skewer was buried in the hill. Try not to disturb the sand.

DATA TABLE

Test	1	2	3	4	5
Width					
Height					

8. Measure and record the sand hill's height and width for Test 1. (See the instructions on the bottom of the previous page to help you accurately measure the height and width.)

9. Now test what happens when you add more sand to the sand hill. Place your cardboard tube vertically at the center of the sand hill. Be careful not to push the tube down into the sand hill! Using the spoon, fill the tube with sand as before.

10. Carefully raise the tube and observe the results of the sand's movement.

11. Measure and record the sand hill's height and width for Test 2.

12. Repeat Steps 9 through 11 at least three more times. After each test, record your results. Be sure to number each test.

Analyze and Conclude

1. Make a graph showing how the sand hill's height and width changed with each test. (*Hint:* Use the *x*-axis of the graph for height. Use the *y*-axis of the graph for width.)

2. What does your graph show about the relationship between the sand hill's height and width?

3. Does your graph support your hypothesis about the sand hill's height and width? Why or why not?

4. How would you revise your original hypothesis after examining your data? Give reasons for your answer.

5. **Think About It** Predict what would happen if you continued the experiment for five more tests. Extend your graph with a dashed line to show your prediction. How could you test your prediction?

Design an Experiment

Do you think the use of different materials, such as wet sand or gravel, would produce different results from dry sand? Make a new hypothesis about the relationship between slope and width in hills made of materials other than dry sand. Design an experiment in which you test how these different materials form hills. Obtain your teacher's approval before you try the experiment.

SECTION 2 Water Erosion

DISCOVER

How Does Moving Water Wear Away Rocks?

1. Obtain two bars of soap that are the same size and brand.

2. Open a faucet just enough to let the water drip out very slowly. How many drops of water does the faucet release per minute?

3. Place one bar of soap in a dry place. Place the other bar of soap under the faucet. Predict the effect of the dripping water droplets on the soap.

4. Let the faucet drip for 10 minutes.

5. Turn off the faucet and observe both bars of soap. What difference do you observe between them?

Think It Over

Predicting What would the bar of soap under the dripping faucet look like if you left it there for another 10 minutes? For an hour? How could you speed up the process? Slow it down?

GUIDE FOR READING

◆ What process is mainly responsible for shaping Earth's land surface?

◆ What features are formed by water erosion?

◆ What features are formed when rivers and streams deposit sediment?

Reading Tip Before you read, use the headings to make an outline on water erosion and deposition.

Walking in the woods in summer, you can hear the racing water of a stream before you see the stream itself. The water roars as it foams over rock ledges and boulders. When you reach the stream, you see water rushing by. Sand and pebbles tumble along the bottom of the stream. As it swirls downstream, it also carries twigs, leaves, and bits of soil. In sheltered pools, insects such as water striders silently skim the water's calm surface. Beneath the surface, you see a rainbow trout hovering in the clear water.

If you visit the stream at other times of year, it will be very different. In winter, the stream freezes. Chunks of ice scrape and grind away at the stream's bed and banks. In spring, the stream floods. Then the flow of water may be strong enough to move large rocks. But throughout the year, the stream continues to erode its small part of Earth's surface.

A woodland stream ▼

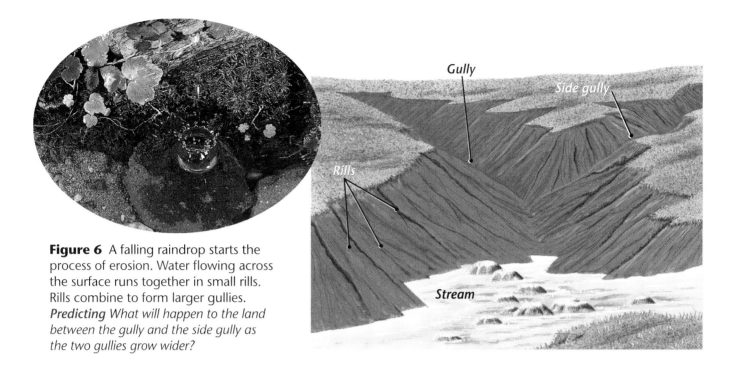

Figure 6 A falling raindrop starts the process of erosion. Water flowing across the surface runs together in small rills. Rills combine to form larger gullies. *Predicting* What will happen to the land between the gully and the side gully as the two gullies grow wider?

Runoff and Erosion

Running water creates many landforms. **Moving water is the major agent of the erosion that has shaped Earth's land surface.**

Erosion by water begins with the splash of rain, as you can see in Figure 6. Some rainfall sinks into the ground. Some evaporates or is taken up by plants. The force of a falling raindrop can loosen and pick up soil particles. As water moves over the land, it carries these particles with it. This moving water is called runoff. **Runoff** is all the remaining water that moves over Earth's surface. When runoff flows in a thin layer over the land, it may cause a type of erosion called sheet erosion.

Rills and Gullies Because of gravity, runoff and the material it contains move downhill. As runoff travels, it forms tiny grooves in the soil called **rills.** As the rills flow into one another, they grow larger, forming gullies. A **gully** is a large groove, or channel, in the soil that carries runoff after a rainstorm. As water flows through gullies, it moves soil and rocks with it, thus enlarging the gullies through erosion. Gullies flow only after it rains.

Figure 7 As water erodes gullies, soil can be lost.

Raindrops Falling

Find out how the force of falling raindrops affects soil.

ACTIVITY

1. Fill a petri dish with fine-textured soil to a depth of about 1 cm. Make sure the soil has a smooth flat surface, but do not pack it firmly in the dish.

2. Place the dish in the center of a newspaper.

3. Fill a dropper with water. Squeeze a large water drop from a height of 1 m onto the surface of the soil. Repeat 4 times.

4. Use a meter stick to measure the distance the soil splashed from the dish. Record your observations.

5. Repeat Steps 1 through 4, this time from a height of 2 m. Which traveled further, the splash from 1 m or the splash from 2 m?

Drawing Conclusions Which test produced the greater amount of erosion? Why?

Streams and Rivers Gullies join together to form a larger channel called a stream. A **stream** is a channel along which water is continually flowing down a slope. Unlike gullies, streams rarely dry up. Small streams are also called creeks or brooks. As streams flow together, they form larger and larger bodies of flowing water. A large stream is often called a **river.**

Amount of Runoff The amount of runoff in an area depends on five main factors. The first factor is the amount of rain an area receives. A second factor is vegetation. Grasses, shrubs, and trees reduce runoff by absorbing water and holding soil in place. A third factor is the type of soil. Some types of soils absorb more water than others. A fourth factor is the shape of the land. Land that is steeply sloped has more runoff than flatter land. Finally, a fifth factor is how people use the land. For instance, a paved parking lot absorbs no water, so all the rain that falls on it becomes runoff. Runoff also increases when a farmer cuts down crops, since this removes vegetation from the land.

Generally, more runoff means more erosion. In contrast, things that reduce runoff, such as plant leaves and roots, will reduce erosion. Even though deserts have little rainfall, they often have high runoff and erosion. This is because deserts usually have few plants. In wet areas, runoff and erosion may be low because there are more plants to protect the soil.

☑ *Checkpoint* What factors affect the amount of runoff in a region?

River Systems

A stream grows into a larger stream or river by receiving water from tributaries. A **tributary** is a stream that flows into a larger stream. A small creek that flows into a large river is a tributary to that river. So too is a large river that adds its water to another large river. For instance, the Missouri River becomes a tributary of the Mississippi River near the city of St. Louis, even though both rivers are about the same size there.

Look at Figure 8. Notice all the tributaries to the Ohio River. Together, all these streams—from tiny rills to great rivers—form a system that drains a large part of eastern North America. A **drainage basin** is the land area from which a river and its tributaries collect their water.

If you were to follow a river upstream all the way to its source, you would finally reach a divide. A **divide** is the high ground between two drainage basins. The most famous divide within the United States is the Continental Divide, which follows the high ground of the Rocky Mountains. The Continental Divide separates streams that flow into the Gulf of Mexico from streams that flow into the Great Basin or the Pacific Ocean.

Erosion by Rivers

Scientists classify rivers by identifying certain features that form as a result of erosion. **Through erosion, a river creates valleys, waterfalls, flood plains, meanders, and oxbow lakes.**

Rivers often form on steep mountain slopes. Near its source, a river is often fast-flowing and generally follows a straight, narrow course. The steep slopes along the river erode rapidly. The result is a deep, V-shaped valley.

Waterfalls may occur where a river meets an area of rock that is very hard and erodes slowly. The river flows over this rock and then flows over softer rock downstream. The softer rock wears away faster than the harder rock. Eventually a waterfall develops where the softer rock was removed. This process formed Niagara Falls, shown in Figure 9. Areas of rough water called rapids also occur where a river tumbles over hard rock.

Ohio River Drainage Basin

Figure 8 The drainage basin of the Ohio River drains much of eastern North America. *Interpreting Maps* What are the tributaries of the Ohio River? Could a tributary come from outside the drainage basin?

Figure 9 Niagara Falls formed on the Niagara River, which connects Lake Erie and Lake Ontario. A flat layer of tough rock lies over a layer of softer rock that erodes easily. When the softer rock erodes, pieces of the harder rock above break off, creating the waterfall's sharp drop.

Harder rock layer

Softer rock layers

Figure 10 The oxbow lake (above) was formerly a part of the channel of the Kasanak River in Alaska. These meanders (right) were formed by a river in Australia.

Lower down on its course, a river usually flows over more gently sloping land. The river spreads out and erodes the land, forming a wide river valley. The flat, wide area of land along a river is a **flood plain.** A river often covers its flood plain when it overflows its banks during floods. On a wide flood plain, the valley walls may be kilometers away from the river itself.

A river often develops meanders where it flows through easily eroded rock or sediment. A **meander** is a looplike bend in the course of a river. As the river widens from side to side, it tends to erode the outer bank and deposit sediment on the inner bank of a bend. Over time, the bend—or meander—becomes more and more curved.

When the gently sloping part of a river flows through an area of sediment or soft rock, it can erode a very wide flood plain. Along this part of a river's course, its channel is deep and wide. Meanders are common along this part of a river. The southern stretch of the Mississippi River is one example of a river that meanders on a wide, gently sloping flood plain.

Sometimes a meandering river forms a feature called an oxbow lake. An **oxbow lake** is a meander that has been cut off from the river. An oxbow lake may form when a river floods. During the flood, high water finds a straighter route downstream. As the flood waters fall, sediments dam up the ends of a meander. The meander has become an oxbow lake.

☑ *Checkpoint* *How does an oxbow lake form?*

Deposits by Rivers

As water moves, it carries sediments with it. Any time moving water slows down, it drops, or deposits, some of the sediment. As the water slows down, fine particles fall to the river's bed. Larger stones quit rolling and sliding. **Deposition creates landforms such as alluvial fans and deltas. It can also add soil to a river's flood plain.** In *Exploring the Course of a River* on pages 78–79, you can see these and other features shaped by rivers and streams.

Alluvial Fans   Where a stream flows out of a steep, narrow mountain valley, the stream suddenly becomes wider and shallower. The water slows down. Here sediments are deposited in an alluvial fan. An **alluvial fan** is a wide, sloping deposit of sediment formed where a stream leaves a mountain range. As its name suggests, this deposit is shaped like a fan.

Deltas   A river ends its journey when it flows into a still body of water, such as an ocean or a lake. Because the river water is no longer flowing downhill, the water slows down. At this point, the sediment in the water drops to the bottom. Sediment deposited where a river flows into an ocean or lake builds up a landform called a **delta.** Deltas can be a variety of shapes: some are arc-shaped, others are triangle-shaped. The delta of the Mississippi River is an example of a type of delta called a "bird's foot" delta.

Soil on Flood Plains   Deposition also occurs during floods.

![Integrating Life Science icon] **INTEGRATING** *LIFE SCIENCE*   Then heavy rains or melting snow cause a river to rise above its banks and spread out over its flood plain. When the flood water finally retreats, it deposits sediment as new soil. Deposition of new soil over a flood plain is what makes a river valley fertile. Dense forests can grow in the rich soil of a flood plain. The soil is also perfect for growing crops.

Figure 11   This alluvial fan in Death Valley, California, was formed from deposits by streams from the mountains.

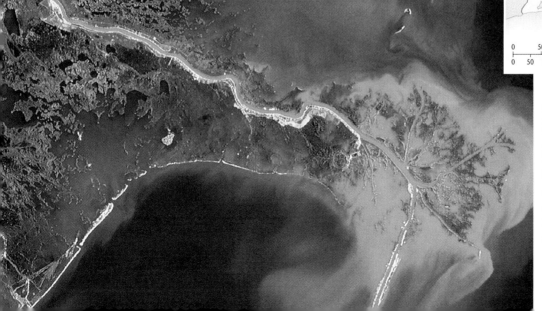

Figure 12   This satellite image shows part of the Mississippi River delta, which is always growing and changing. *Observing What happens to the Mississippi River as it flows through its delta? Can you find the river's main channel?*

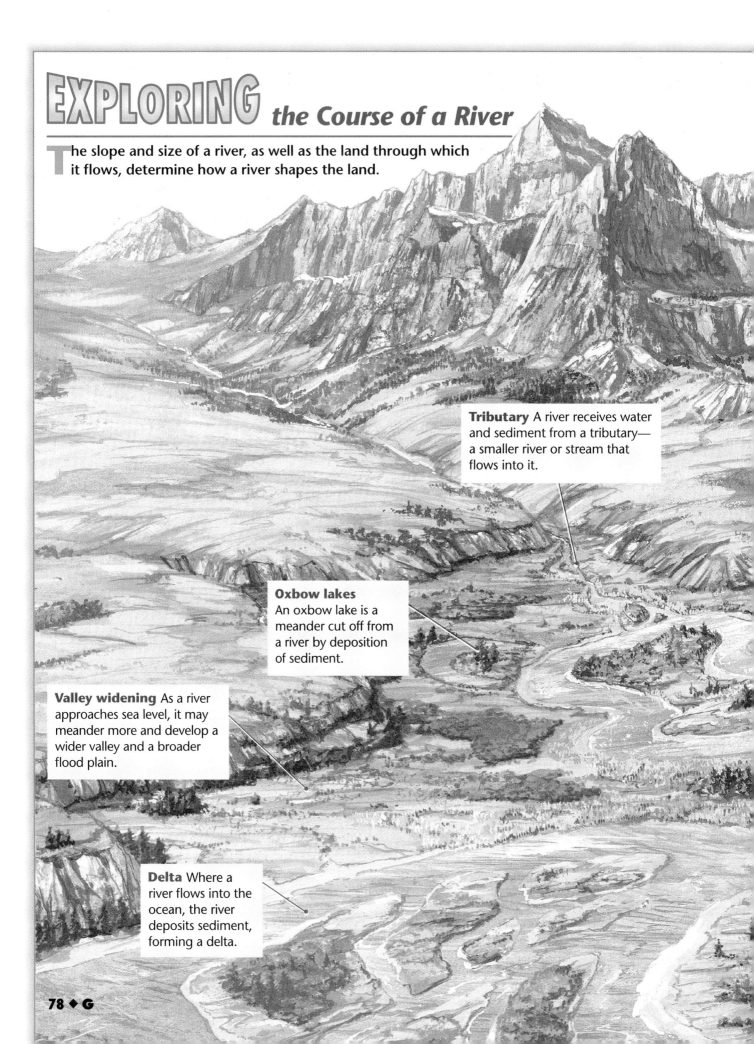

EXPLORING *the Course of a River*

The slope and size of a river, as well as the land through which it flows, determine how a river shapes the land.

Tributary A river receives water and sediment from a tributary—a smaller river or stream that flows into it.

Oxbow lakes
An oxbow lake is a meander cut off from a river by deposition of sediment.

Valley widening As a river approaches sea level, it may meander more and develop a wider valley and a broader flood plain.

Delta Where a river flows into the ocean, the river deposits sediment, forming a delta.

Waterfalls and rapids
Waterfalls and rapids are common where the river passes over harder rock.

V-shaped valley
Near its source, a river often flows through a deep, V-shaped valley. As the river flows, it cuts a deeper valley.

Meanders Where a river flows across easily eroded sediment, its channel bends from side to side in a series of meanders.

Oxbow lake

Flood plain A flood plain forms when a river's power of erosion widens its valley rather than deepening it.

Beaches Sand carried downstream by rivers spreads along the coast to form beaches.

Groundwater Erosion and Deposition

When rain falls and snow melts, not all of the water evaporates or becomes runoff. Some water soaks into the ground. There it fills the openings in the soil and trickles into cracks and spaces in layers of rock. **Groundwater** is the term geologists use for this underground water. Like running water on the surface, groundwater affects the shape of the land.

INTEGRATING CHEMISTRY Groundwater can cause erosion through a process of chemical weathering. When water sinks into the ground, it combines with carbon dioxide to form a weak acid, called carbonic acid. Carbonic acid can break down limestone. Groundwater containing carbonic acid flows into cracks in the limestone. Then some of the limestone changes chemically and is carried away in a solution of water. This gradually hollows out pockets in the rock. Over time, these pockets develop into large holes underground, called caves or caverns.

The action of carbonic acid on limestone can also result in deposition. Inside limestone caves, deposits called stalactites and stalagmites often form. Water containing carbonic acid and calcium from limestone drips from a cave's roof. As the water

Figure 13 Over millions of years, chemical weathering of limestone and groundwater erosion created the beautiful shapes in Carlsbad Caverns in New Mexico.
Interpreting Photos What evidence of deposition do you see in the photo of Carlsbad Caverns?

Figure 14 A sinkhole, such as this one in Florida, is a characteristic feature of karst topography. Sinkholes can pose a hazard for people who live in a karst region.

evaporates, a deposit of calcite forms. A deposit that hangs like an icicle from the roof of a cave is called a **stalactite** (stuh LAK tyt). Slow dripping builds up a cone-shaped **stalagmite** (stuh LAG myt) from the cave floor.

In rainy regions where there is a layer of limestone near the surface, groundwater erosion can significantly change the shape of the land. Streams are rare, because water sinks easily down into the weathered limestone. Deep valleys and caverns are common. If the roof of a cave collapses because of the erosion of the underlying limestone, the result is a depression called a sinkhole. This type of landscape is called **karst topography** after a region in Eastern Europe. In the United States, there are regions of karst topography in Florida, Kentucky, and Indiana.

Section 2 Review

1. What is the major cause of erosion on Earth's surface?
2. Briefly describe five features formed by rivers and streams as they erode the land.
3. What are the results of deposition along the course of a stream or river?
4. How can groundwater contribute to erosion?
5. **Thinking Critically Comparing and Contrasting** How is an alluvial fan similar to a delta? How is it different?

Science at Home

In a small dish, build a cube out of 27 small sugar cubes. Your cube should be three sugar cubes on a side. Fold a square piece of paper towel to fit the top of the cube. Wet the paper towel, place it on the cube, and let it stand for 15 or 20 minutes. Every few minutes, sprinkle a few drops of water on the paper towel to keep it wet. Then remove the paper towel. What happened to your cube? How is the effect of water on a sugar cube similar to groundwater eroding limestone? How is it different?

Streams in Action

Erosion can form gullies, wash away topsoil, and pollute rivers with sediment. You can observe the effects of erosion using a stream table.

Problem

How do rivers and streams erode the land?

Skills Focus

making models, observing, predicting

Materials

plastic tub at least 27 cm × 40 cm × 10 cm

diatomaceous earth   plastic measuring cup

spray bottle   hand lens

watch or clock   water

1 metal spoon   plastic foam cup

blue food coloring   liquid detergent

scissors

2 wood blocks about 2.5 cm thick

bucket to hold 2–3 L of water or a source of tap water

plastic stirrers, 10–12 cm long, with two small holes each

wire 13–15 cm long, 20 gauge

Procedure

Part A Creating Streams Over Time

1. Your teacher will give you a plastic tub containing diatomaceous earth that has been soaked with water. Place the tub on a level surface. **CAUTION:** *Dry diatomaceous earth produces dust that may be irritating if inhaled. To keep the diatomaceous earth from drying out, spray it lightly with water.*

Making the Dripper

1. Insert the wire into one of the two holes in a plastic stirrer. The ends of the wire should protrude from the stirrer.
2. Gently bend the stirrer into a U shape. Be careful not to make any sharp bends. This is the dripper.
3. With scissors, carefully cut two small notches on opposite sides of the top of the foam cup.
4. Fill the cup to just below the notches with water colored with two drops of blue food coloring. Add more food coloring later as you add more water to the cup.
5. Add one drop of detergent to keep air bubbles out of the dripper and increase flow.
6. To start the dripper, fill it with water. Then quickly tip it and place it in one of the notches in the cup, as shown above.
7. Adjust the flow rate of the dripper to about 2 drips per 1 second. (*Hint:* Bend the dripper into more of a U shape to increase flow. Lessen the curve to reduce flow.)

2. One end of the tub will contain more diatomaceous earth. Use the block of wood to raise this end of the tub 2.5 cm.
3. Place the cup at the upper end of the slope with the notches pointing to the left and right.
4. Press the cup firmly down into the earth to secure its position.
5. Start the dripper (see Step 6 in the box above). Allow the water to drip to the right onto the diatomaceous earth.

6. Allow the dripper to drip for 5 minutes. (*Hint:* When you need to add more water, be careful not to disturb the dripper.)
7. Observe the flow of water and the changes it makes. Use the hand lens to look closely at the stream bed.
8. After 5 minutes, remove the dripper.
9. In your lab notebook, draw a picture of the resulting stream and label it "5 minutes."
10. Now switch the dripper to the left side of the cup. Restart the dripper and allow it to drip for 10 minutes. Then remove the dripper.
11. Draw a picture and label it "10 minutes."

Part B Changing the Angle of Slope
1. Remove the cup from the stream table.
2. Save the stream bed on the right side of the tub. Using the bowl of the spoon, smooth out the diatomaceous earth on the left side.
3. To increase the angle of slope of your stream table, raise the end of the tub another 2.5 cm.

4. In your lab notebook, predict the effects of increasing the angle of slope.
5. Replace the cup and restart the dripper, placing it in the notch on the left side of the cup. Allow the dripper to drip for 5 minutes. Notice any changes in the new stream bed.
6. At the end of 5 minutes, remove the dripper.
7. Draw a picture of the new stream bed in your lab notebook. Label it "Increased Angle."
8. Follow your teacher's instructions for clean-up after this activity. Wash your hands when you have finished.

Analyze and Conclude

1. Compare the 5-minute stream with the 10-minute stream. How did the length of time that the water flowed affect erosion along the stream bed?
2. Were your predictions about the effects of increasing the angle of slope correct? Explain your answer.
3. What eventually happened to the eroded material that was carried downstream?
4. What other variables besides time and angle of slope might affect the way rivers and streams erode the land?
5. **Apply** Have you ever seen water flowing down a hillside or street after a heavy rain? If so, how much did the land slope in that area? Did you notice anything about the color of the water? Explain.

Design an Experiment

Design a stream table experiment to measure how the amount of sediment carried by a river changes as the volume of flow of the river increases. Obtain your teacher's approval before you try the experiment.

Protecting Homes in Flood Plains

At least ten million American households are located in flood plains. Living near a river is tempting. Riverside land is often flat and easy to build on. Because so many people now live in flood plains, the cost of flood damage has been growing. Communities along rivers want to limit the cost of flooding. They want to know how they can protect the people and buildings already in flood plains. They also want to know how to discourage more people from moving into flood plains.

The Issues

Should the Government Insure People Against Flood Damage? The United States government offers insurance to households in flood plains. The insurance pays part of the cost of repairs after a flood. Insurance helps people, but it is very expensive. Only 17 percent of people who live in flood plains buy the government insurance. Government flood insurance is available only in places that take steps to reduce flood damage. Cities must allow new building only on high ground. The insurance will not pay to rebuild homes that are badly damaged by floodwater. Instead, these people must use the money to find a home somewhere else.

Critics say that insurance just encourages people to move back into areas that flood. Supporters say it rewards towns and cities that make rules to control building on flood plains.

How Much of the Flood Plain Should Be Protected? Government flood insurance is available only in areas where scientists expect flooding about once in 100 years, or once in 500 years. Such figures are just estimates. Three floods occurred in only 12 years in a government flood-insurance area near Sacramento, California.

Should the Government Tell People Where They Can Live? Some programs of flood control forbid all new building. Other programs may also encourage people to move to safer areas. The 1997 flood on the Red River in Grand Forks, North Dakota, is one example. After the flood, the city of Grand Forks offered to buy all the damaged buildings near the river. The city wants to build high walls of earth to protect the rest of the town.

The Grand Forks plan might prevent future damage, but is it fair? Supporters say that since the government has to pay for flood damage, it has the right to make people leave flood plains. Critics of such plans say that people should be free to live where they want, even in risky areas.

Who should decide in which neighborhood no new houses can be built? Who decides which people should be asked to move away from a flood plain? Experts disagree over whether local, state, or United States government officials should decide which areas to include. Some believe scientists should make the decision.

You Decide

1. Identify the Problem
In your own words, describe the controversy surrounding flood plains and housing.

2. Analyze the Options
List several steps that could be taken to reduce the damage done to buildings in flood plains. For each step, include who would benefit from the step, and who would pay the costs.

3. Find a Solution
Your town has to decide what to do about a neighborhood damaged by the worst flood in 50 years. Write a speech that argues for your solution.

SECTION 3 The Force of Moving Water

DISCOVER ·····················

How Are Sediments Deposited?

1. Put on your goggles.

2. Obtain a clear plastic jar or bottle with a top. Fill the jar about two-thirds full with water.

3. Fill a plastic beaker with 200 mL of fine and coarse sand, soil, clay, and small pebbles.

4. Pour the mixture into the jar of water. Screw on the top tightly and shake for two minutes. Be sure to hold onto the jar firmly.

5. Set the jar down and observe it for 10 to 15 minutes.

Think It Over

Inferring In what order are the sediments in the jar deposited? What do you think causes this pattern?

The Merrimack River in New Hampshire and Massachusetts is only 180 kilometers long. But the Merrimack does a great deal of work as it runs from the mountains to the sea. The river's waters fall 82 meters through many rapids and waterfalls. During the 1800s, people harnessed this falling water to run machines. These machines could spin thread and weave cloth very quickly and cheaply. Thanks to water power, the towns along the river grew quickly into cities.

Work and Energy

The waters of the Merrimack River could drive machines because a river's water has energy. **Energy** is the ability to do work or cause change. There are two kinds of energy. **Potential energy** is energy that is stored and waiting to be used later. The Merrimack's waters begin with potential energy due to their position above sea level. **Kinetic energy** is the energy an object has due to its motion. **As gravity pulls water down a slope, the water's potential energy changes to kinetic energy that can do work.**

GUIDE FOR READING

◆ What enables water to do work?

◆ How does sediment enter rivers and streams?

◆ What factors affect a river's ability to erode and carry sediment?

Reading Tip Before you read, rewrite the headings of the section as *how, why,* or *what* questions. As you read, look for answers to these questions.

Figure 15 Dams like this one on the Merrimack River in Lowell, Massachusetts, help to harness the power of flowing water.

The cotton mills in Lowell, Massachusetts, were built in the 1820s. The mills employed young women from the farms and small towns of New England. At that time, it was unusual for women to work outside the home. The hours of work at a mill were long and pay was low. But mill work helped these women to earn and save their own money. Most later returned to their hometowns.

In Your Journal

Use library references to find out more about the daily life of the mill workers. Write a diary entry describing a worker's typical day.

When energy does work, the energy is transferred from one object to another. At the textile mills along the Merrimack River, the kinetic energy of the moving water was transferred to the spinning machines. It became mechanical energy harnessed for a human purpose—making cloth. But all along a river, kinetic energy does other work. A river is always moving sediment from the mountains to the sea. At the same time, a river is also eroding its banks and valley.

☑ *Checkpoint* What are potential energy and kinetic energy?

How Water Erodes and Carries Sediment

Gravity causes the movement of water across Earth's land surface. But how does water cause erosion? In the process of water erosion, water picks up and moves sediment. Sediment includes soil, rock, clay, and sand. Sediment can enter rivers and streams in a number of ways. **Most sediment washes or falls into the river as a result of mass movement and runoff. Other sediment erodes from the bottom or sides of the river.** Wind may also drop sediment into the water.

Abrasion is another process by which a river obtains sediment. **Abrasion** is the wearing away of rock by a grinding action. Abrasion occurs when particles of sediment in flowing water bump into the streambed again and again. Abrasion grinds down sediment particles. For example, boulders become smaller as they are moved down a streambed. Sediments also grind and chip away at the rock of the streambed, deepening and widening the stream's channel.

The amount of sediment that a river carries is its **load.** Gravity and the force of the moving water cause the sediment load to move downstream. Most large sediment falls to the bottom and moves by rolling and sliding. Fast-moving water actually lifts sand and other, smaller, sediment and carries it downstream. Water dissolves some sediment completely. The river carries these dissolved sediments in solution. If you look at Figure 16, you can observe the different ways in which water can carry sediment. Notice for example, how grains of sand or small stones can move by bouncing.

Figure 16 Rivers and streams carry sediment in several ways. *Predicting What will eventually happen to a boulder on the bottom of a river?*

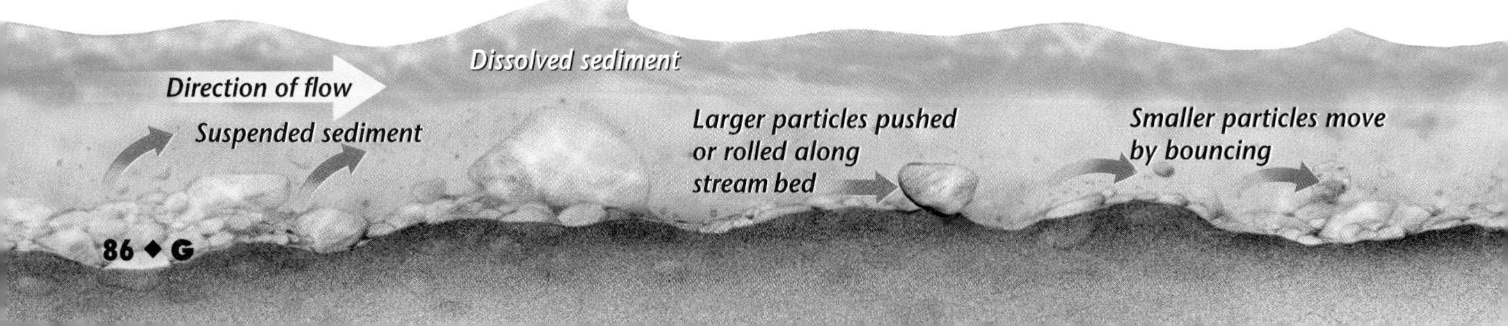

Direction of flow

Dissolved sediment

Suspended sediment

Larger particles pushed or rolled along stream bed

Smaller particles move by bouncing

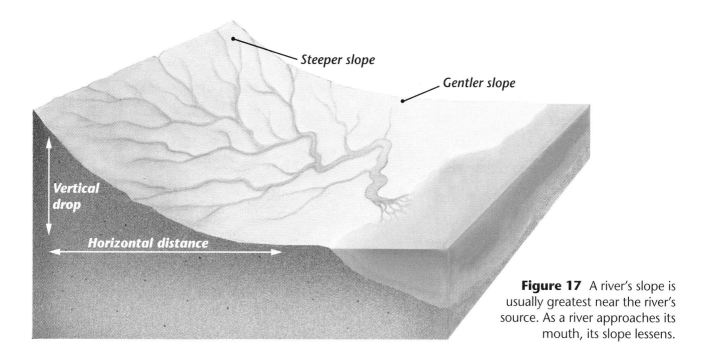

Steeper slope

Gentler slope

Vertical drop

Horizontal distance

Figure 17 A river's slope is usually greatest near the river's source. As a river approaches its mouth, its slope lessens.

Erosion and Sediment Load

The power of a river to cause erosion and carry sediment depends on several factors. **A river's slope, volume of flow, and the shape of its streambed all affect how fast the river flows and how much sediment it can erode.**

A fast-flowing river carries more and larger particles of sediment. When a river slows down, its sediment load is deposited. The larger particles of sediment are deposited first.

Slope Generally, if a river's slope increases, the water's speed also increases. A river's slope is the amount the river drops toward sea level over a given distance. If a river's speed increases, its sediment load and power to erode may increase. But other factors are also important in determining how much sediment the river erodes and carries.

Volume of Flow A river's flow is the volume of water that moves past a point on the river in a given time. As more water flows through a river, its speed increases. During a flood, the increased volume of water helps the river to cut more deeply into its banks and bed. A flooding river may have hundreds of times more eroding power than the river has at other times. A flooding river can carry huge amounts of sand, soil, and other sediments. It may move giant boulders as if they were pebbles.

Streambed Shape A streambed's shape affects the amount of friction between the water and the streambed. **Friction** is the force that opposes the motion of one surface as it moves across another surface. Friction, in turn, affects a river's speed. Where a river is deep, less water comes in contact with the streambed. This reduces

Developing Hypotheses

A geologist is **ACTIVITY** comparing alluvial fans. One alluvial fan is composed of gravel and small boulders. The other fan is composed of sand and silt. Propose a hypothesis to explain the difference in the size of the particles in the two fans. (*Hint*: Think of the characteristics of the streams that formed each alluvial fan.)

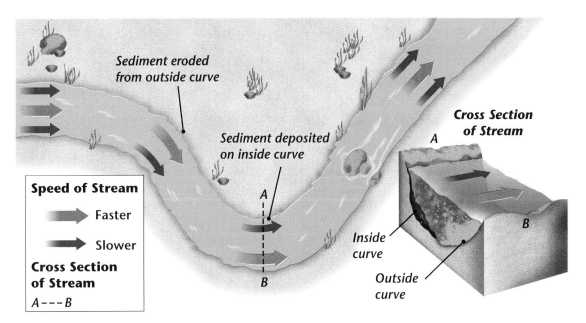

Sediment eroded
from outside curve

Sediment deposited
on inside curve

**Cross Section
of Stream**

A

B

*Inside
curve*

*Outside
curve*

Speed of Stream

→ Faster

→ Slower

**Cross Section
of Stream**

A - - - B

Figure 18 A river erodes sediment from its banks on the outside curve and deposits its sediment on the inside curve.
Relating Cause and Effect Why does a river deposit sediment on the inside of a curve?

friction and allows the river to flow faster. In a shallow river, much of the water comes in contact with the streambed. Therefore friction increases, reducing the river's speed.

A streambed is often full of boulders and other obstacles. This roughness prevents the water from flowing smoothly. Roughness thus increases friction and reduces the river's speed. Instead of moving downstream, the water moves every which way in a type of movement called **turbulence.** For example, a stream on a steep slope may flow at a lower speed than a large river on a gentle slope. Friction and turbulence slow the stream's flow. But a turbulent stream or river may have great power to erode.

The shape of a river affects the way it deposits sediment. Where a river flows in a straight line, the water flows faster near the center of the river than along its sides. Deposition occurs along the sides of the river, where the water moves more slowly.

If a river curves, the water moves fastest along the outside of the curve. There, the river tends to cut into its bank. Sediment is deposited on the inside curve, where the water speed is slowest. You can see this process in Figure 18.

 Section 3 Review

1. How can moving water on Earth's surface do work?
2. How does a river collect sediment?
3. What are three factors that affect a river's sediment load?
4. Describe three ways that sediment moves in a river.
5. **Thinking Critically Relating Cause and Effect** What effect does increased slope have on a river's speed and sediment load? Explain.

CHAPTER
PROJECT
3

Check Your Progress
Make a drawing of the landscape that you plan to model. This landscape will show the land before erosion. What kinds of landforms will you show in the model? Be sure to include a high mountain and a coastline. Make a list of materials that you will use to build your model. Once your teacher has approved your drawing and your list of materials, you may build your first model.

SECTION
4 Glaciers

DISCOVER • ACTIVITY

How Do Glaciers Change the Land?

1. Put some sand in a small plastic container.

2. Fill the container with water and place the container in a freezer until the water turns to ice.

3. Remove the block of ice from the container.

4. Holding the ice with paper towels, rub the ice, sand side down, over a bar of soap. Observe what happens to the surface of the soap.

Think It Over

Inferring Based on your observations, how do you think moving ice could change the surface of the land?

You are on a boat trip near the coast of Alaska. You sail by vast evergreen forests and snow-capped mountains. Then, as your boat rounds a point of land, you see an amazing sight. A great mass of ice winds like a river between rows of mountains. Suddenly you hear a noise like thunder. Where the ice meets the sea, a giant chunk of ice breaks off and plunges into the water. Carefully, you pilot your boat around the iceberg and toward the mass of ice. It towers over your boat. You see that it is made up of solid ice that is deep blue and green as well as white. What is this river of ice?

GUIDE FOR READING

◆ What are the two kinds of glaciers?

◆ How do glaciers cause erosion and deposition?

Reading Tip Before you read, preview the headings and key terms in the section. Make a list of predictions about the characteristics of glaciers.

Kinds of Glaciers

Geologists define a **glacier** as any large mass of ice that moves slowly over land. **There are two kinds of glaciers—valley glaciers and continental glaciers.**

A **valley glacier** is a long, narrow glacier that forms when snow and ice build up high in a mountain valley. The sides of mountains keep these glaciers from spreading out in all directions. Instead, they usually move down valleys that have already been cut by rivers. Valley glaciers are found on many high mountains.

A **continental glacier** is a glacier that covers much of a continent or large island. Continental glaciers are much larger than

Figure 19 The Mendenhall Glacier in Alaska winds downhill between high mountains.

G ◆ 89

The Ice Age in North America

KEY
Area covered by
continental glacier

Figure 20 The continental glacier of the last ice age covered most of Canada and Alaska as well as much of the northern United States. The ice age lasted about 70,000 years and ended about 10,000 years ago.

valley glaciers. They spread out over large areas of the land. Today, continental glaciers cover about 10 percent of Earth's land. They cover Antarctica and most of Greenland. The glacier covering Antarctica spreads out over 14 million square kilometers and is over 2 kilometers thick.

Ice Ages

Many times in the past, continental glaciers have covered large parts of Earth's surface. These times are known as **ice ages.** For example, about 9 million years ago, continental glaciers began to form in North America, Europe, and Asia. These glaciers slowly grew and advanced southward. By about 2.5 million years ago, they covered about a third of Earth's land. The glaciers advanced and retreated, or melted back, several times. Figure 20 shows how far south the glaciers came on the North American continent during the most recent ice age. They finally retreated about 10,000 years ago.

How Glaciers Form and Move

Glaciers can form only in an area where more snow falls than melts. High in mountain valleys, temperatures seldom rise above freezing. Snow builds up year after year. The pressure of the weight of more and more snow compacts the snow at the bottom into ice. Once the depth of snow and ice reaches more than 30 to 40 meters, gravity begins to pull the glacier downhill.

Valley glaciers flow at a rate of a few centimeters to a few meters per day. But sometimes a valley glacier slides down more quickly in what is called a surge. A surging glacier can flow as much as 6 kilometers a year. Unlike valley glaciers, continental glaciers can flow in all directions. Continental glaciers spread out much as pancake batter spreads out in a frying pan.

☑ *Checkpoint* How do glaciers form?

Glacial Erosion

The movement of a glacier changes the land beneath it. Although glaciers work slowly, they are a major force of erosion. **The two processes by which glaciers erode the land are plucking and abrasion.**

As a glacier flows over the land, it picks up rocks in a process called **plucking.** Beneath a glacier, the weight of the ice can break rocks apart. These rock fragments freeze to the bottom of the glacier. When the glacier moves, it carries the rocks with it. Figure 21 shows plucking by a glacier. Plucking can move even huge boulders.

Many rocks remain on the bottom of the glacier, and the glacier drags them across the land. This process, called abrasion, gouges and scratches the bedrock. You can see the results of erosion by glaciers in *Exploring Glacial Landforms* on pages 92–93.

Glacial Deposition

A glacier gathers a huge amount of rock and soil as it erodes the land in its path. **When a glacier melts, it deposits the sediment it eroded from the land, creating various landforms.** These landforms remain for thousands of years after the glacier has melted.

The mixture of sediments that a glacier deposits directly on the surface is called **till.** Till is made up of particles of many different sizes. Clay, silt, sand, gravel, and boulders can all be found in till.

The till deposited at the edges of a glacier forms a ridge called a **moraine.** A terminal moraine is the ridge of till at the farthest point reached by a glacier. Long Island in New York is a terminal moraine from the continental glaciers of the last ice age.

INTEGRATING LIFE SCIENCE Other features left in glacial sediments are prairie potholes. These potholes are shallow depressions in till that were formed by flowing water as the continental glacier melted. Today, prairie potholes contain water for only part of the year. Each prairie pothole is a small oasis for living things. Grasses and moisture-loving plants grow thickly in and around the potholes. In the spring, the potholes brim with water from melting snow or rain. Thousands of migrating ducks and other birds stop off at the potholes to feed and rest on their way north. Some stay to build nests and raise their young.

Figure 21 As a glacier moves downhill, the ice plucks pieces of bedrock from the ground. *Predicting What evidence of plucking might you find after a glacier melts?*

Figure 22 This prairie pothole in Wisconsin is surrounded by farmland. Prairie potholes were left in till deposited by glaciers.

EXPLORING *Glacial Landforms*

As glaciers advance and retreat, they sculpt the landscape by erosion and deposition.

Horn When glaciers carve away the sides of a mountain, the result is a horn, a sharpened peak.

Cirque A cirque is a bowl-shaped hollow eroded by a glacier.

Arête An arête is a sharp ridge separating two cirques.

Fiord A fiord forms when the level of the sea rises, filling a valley once cut by a glacier in a coastal region.

Retreating glaciers also create features called kettles. A **kettle** is a small depression that forms when a chunk of ice is left in glacial till. When the ice melts, the kettle remains. The continental glacier of the last ice age left behind many kettles. Kettles often fill with water, forming small ponds or lakes called kettle lakes. Such lakes are common in areas that were covered with ice.

The continental glacier of the last ice age also formed the Great Lakes. Before the ice age, there were large river valleys in the area now occupied by the lakes. As the ice advanced over these valleys, it scooped out loose sediment and soft rock, forming broad, deep basins. The Great Lakes formed over thousands of years as the glaciers melted and these basins filled with water.

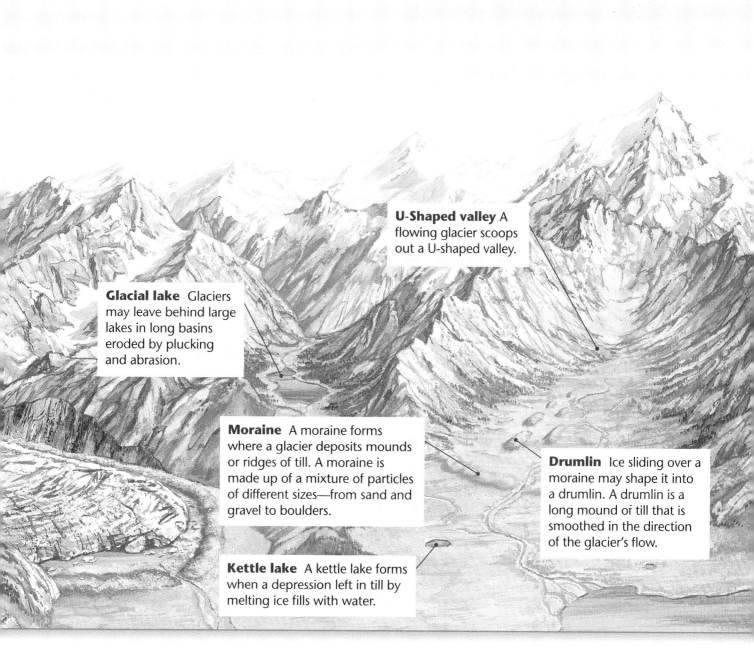

U-Shaped valley A flowing glacier scoops out a U-shaped valley.

Glacial lake Glaciers may leave behind large lakes in long basins eroded by plucking and abrasion.

Moraine A moraine forms where a glacier deposits mounds or ridges of till. A moraine is made up of a mixture of particles of different sizes—from sand and gravel to boulders.

Drumlin Ice sliding over a moraine may shape it into a drumlin. A drumlin is a long mound of till that is smoothed in the direction of the glacier's flow.

Kettle lake A kettle lake forms when a depression left in till by melting ice fills with water.

 Section 4 Review

1. How are valley glaciers and continental glaciers different?
2. What are two types of glacial erosion?
3. Describe three features formed by glacial deposition.
4. **Thinking Critically Relating Cause and Effect** Driving through the countryside in Michigan, you and your family come upon a series of small, round lakes. Explain the process that formed these features.

Check Your Progress

CHAPTER PROJECT 3

Now you are ready to begin building your second model. Pattern the model after your drawing that predicts the effects of erosion and deposition. The model will show how gravity, water, and glaciers have changed your model landscape. Where on your model would glaciers be likely to form?

⑤ Waves

What Can Be Learned From Beach Sand?

1. Collect a spoonful of sand from each of two different beaches. The two samples also may come from different parts of the same beach.

2. Examine the first sample of beach sand with a hand lens.

3. Record the properties of the sand grains, for example, color and shape. Are the grains smooth and rounded or angular and rough? Are all the grains in the sample the same shape and color?

4. Examine the second sample and repeat Step 3. How do the two samples compare?

Think It Over

Posing Questions What questions do you need to answer to understand beach sand? Use what you know about erosion and deposition to help you think of questions.

GUIDE FOR READING

◆ What gives waves their energy?

◆ How do waves shape a coast?

Reading Tip As you read, make a concept map showing features formed by wave erosion and deposition.

Ocean waves contain energy—sometimes a great deal of energy. The waves that sweep onto the Pacific coast are especially powerful. Created by ocean winds, they carry energy vast distances across the Pacific Ocean. Acting like drills or buzzsaws, the waves erode the solid rock of the coast into cliffs and caves. Waves also carry sediment that forms features such as beaches. But these features do not last long. More waves follow to change the shoreline yet again.

How Waves Form

The energy in waves comes from wind that blows across the water's surface. As the wind makes contact with the water, some of its energy transfers to the water. Large ocean waves are the result of powerful storms far out at sea. But ordinary breezes can produce waves in lakes or small ponds.

The energy that water picks up from the wind causes water particles to move up and down as the wave goes by. But the water particles themselves don't move forward. Only the form of the wave moves. Have you ever watched a wave in a field of tall grass? Each blade of grass moves back and forth but doesn't move from its place. But the energy of the wave moves across the field.

Waves on the Oregon coast ▼

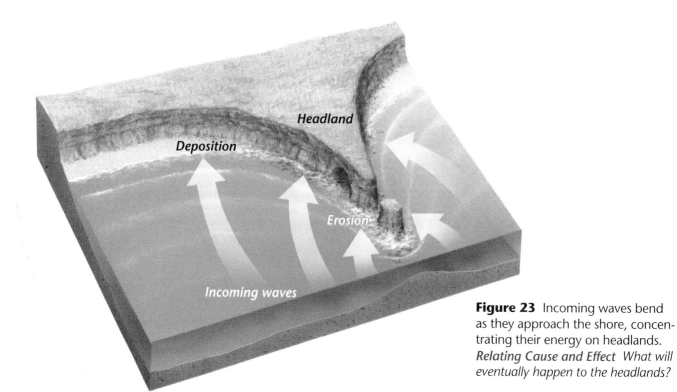

Headland

Deposition

Erosion

Incoming waves

Figure 23 Incoming waves bend as they approach the shore, concentrating their energy on headlands. *Relating Cause and Effect What will eventually happen to the headlands?*

A wave changes as it approaches land. In deep water, a wave only affects the water near the surface. But as the wave approaches shallow water, the wave begins to drag the bottom. The friction between the wave and the bottom causes the wave to slow down. Now the water actually does move forward with the wave. This forward-moving water provides the force that shapes the land along the shoreline.

Erosion by Waves

Waves are the major force of erosion along coasts. One way waves erode the land is by impact. Large waves can hit rocks along the shore with great force. This energy in waves can break apart rocks. Over time, waves can make small cracks larger. Eventually, the waves cause pieces of rock to break off.

Waves also erode land by abrasion. As a wave approaches shallow water, it picks up sediment, including sand and gravel. This sediment is carried forward by the wave. When the wave hits land, the sediment wears away rock like sandpaper wearing away wood.

Waves coming to shore gradually change direction. The change in direction occurs as different parts of a wave begin to drag on the bottom. Notice how the waves in Figure 23 change direction as they approach the shore. The energy of these waves is concentrated on headlands. A headland is a part of the shore that sticks out into the ocean. Headlands stand out from the coast because they are made of harder rock that resists the waves. But, over time, waves erode the headlands and even out the shoreline.

✓ *Checkpoint What are two of the processes by which waves can cause erosion?*

Calculating

A sandy coast erodes at a rate of 1.25 meters per year. But a severe storm can erode an additional 3.75 meters from the shore. If 12 severe storms occur during a 50-year period, how much will the coast erode? If you wish, you may use an electronic calculator to find the answer.

Figure 24 Waves cut these cliffs on the coast of Australia. The blocks of rock offshore are sea stacks. *Developing Hypotheses Develop a hypothesis to explain how these sea stacks formed.*

Landforms Created by Wave Erosion

When waves hit a steep, rocky coast, they strike the area again and again. Think of an ax striking the trunk of a tree. The cut gets bigger and deeper with each strike of the blade. Finally the tree falls. In a similar way, ocean waves erode the base of the land along a steep coast. Where the rock is softer, the waves erode the land faster. Over time the waves may erode a hollow area in the rock called a sea cave.

Eventually, waves may erode the base of a cliff so much that the rock above collapses. The result is a wave-cut cliff. You can see an example of such a cliff in Figure 24.

Another feature created by wave erosion is a sea arch. A sea arch forms when waves erode a layer of softer rock that underlies a layer of harder rock. If an arch collapses, the result might be a sea stack, a pillar of rock rising above the water.

Checkpoint How can waves produce a cliff on a rocky coast?

Deposits by Waves

Waves not only erode the land, they also deposit sediment. **Waves shape the coast through both erosion and deposition.** Deposition occurs when waves slow down and the water drops its sediment. This process is similar to the deposition that occurs on a river delta when the river slows down and drops its sediment load.

As waves reach the shore, they drop the sediment they carry, forming a beach. A **beach** is an area of wave-washed sediment along a coast. The sediment deposited on beaches is usually sand. Most sand comes from rivers that carry eroded particles of rock into the ocean. But not all beaches are made of sand carried by rivers. Some beaches are made of small fragments of coral or sea shells piled up by wave action. Florida has many such beaches.

The sediment on a beach usually moves down the beach after it has been deposited. Waves usually hit the beach at an angle instead of straight on. These angled waves create a current that runs parallel to the coastline. As repeated waves hit the beach, some of the beach sediment moves down the beach with the current, in a process called **longshore drift.**

One result of longshore drift is the formation of a spit. A **spit** is a beach that projects like a finger out into the water. Spits form as a result of deposition by longshore drift. Spits occur where a headland or other obstacle interrupts longshore drift, or where the coast turns abruptly. Incoming waves carrying sand may build up sandbars, long ridges of sand parallel to the shore.

 INTEGRATING A barrier beach is similar to a *ENVIRONMENTAL SCIENCE* sandbar, but a barrier beach forms when storm waves pile up sand above sea level. Barrier beaches are found in many places along the Atlantic coast of the United States, such as the Outer Banks of North Carolina. People have built homes on many of these barrier beaches. But the storm waves that build up the beaches can also wash them away. Barrier beach communities must be prepared for the damage that hurricanes and other storms can bring.

Figure 25 This satellite image of Cape Cod in Massachusetts shows how longshore drift can carry sand and deposit it to form a spit. *Observing* How many spits can you find in this image?

Section 5 Review

1. How do ocean waves form?
2. Describe two landforms created by wave erosion and two landforms created by wave deposition.
3. Why are headlands eroded faster than the land at the ends of inlets and bays?
4. **Thinking Critically Predicting** You visit a rocky headland by the ocean that has a sea arch and several sea stacks. How might this area change in the next 500 years?

Check Your Progress

CHAPTER PROJECT 3

Now you are ready to add the effects of wave erosion to your model. What landforms will wave erosion produce along the coastline on your model? What materials will you use to model these landforms? When you have finished your second model, make labels for the landforms on your models.

SECTION
6 Wind

DISCOVER ·· ACTIVITY····

How Does Moving Air Affect Sediment?

1. Cover the bottom of a pan with a flat layer of cornmeal 1–2 centimeters deep.

2. Gently blow over the layer of cornmeal using a straw to direct your breath. Observe what happens.

CAUTION: *Do not blow the cornmeal in the direction of another student.*

Think It Over

Observing What changes did the wind you created make in the flat layer of cornmeal?

GUIDE FOR READING

◆ How does wind cause erosion?

◆ What features result from deposition by wind?

Reading Tip Before you read, preview Figure 27. In your notebook, write some predictions about the characteristics of wind erosion.

Imagine a landscape made almost entirely of sand. One such place is the Namib Desert. The desert stretches for about 1,900 kilometers along the coast of Namibia in Africa. In the southern half of the Namib are long rows of giant sand dunes. A **sand dune** is a deposit of wind-blown sand. Some sand dunes in the Namib are more than 200 meters high and 15 kilometers long. Much of the sand in the dunes originally came from the nearby Orange River. Over thousands of years, wind has swept the sand across the desert, piling up huge, ever-changing dunes.

How Wind Causes Erosion

Wind by itself is the weakest agent of erosion. Water, waves, moving ice, and even mass movement have more effect on the land. Yet wind can be a powerful force in shaping the land in areas where there are few plants to hold the soil in place. As you might guess, wind is very effective in causing erosion in deserts. There few plants can grow, and wind can easily move the grains of dry, light sand.

Figure 26 Wind erosion continues to shape the giant sand dunes in the Namib Desert along Africa's southwestern coast.

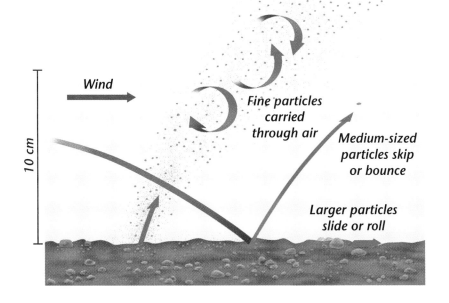

Wind

Fine particles
carried
through air

Medium-sized
particles skip
or bounce

Larger particles
slide or roll

10 cm

Figure 27 Wind erosion moves sediment particles of different sizes in the three ways shown above. *Comparing and Contrasting Compare the movement of sediment by wind with the movement of sediment by water in Figure 16 on page 86. How are the processes similar? How are they different?*

The main way that wind causes erosion is by deflation. Geologists define **deflation** as the process by which wind removes surface materials. When wind blows over the land, it picks up the smallest particles of sediment. This sediment is made of bits of clay and silt. The stronger the wind, the larger the particles that it can pick up and move through the air. Slightly heavier particles, such as sand, might skip or bounce for a short distance. But sand soon falls back to the ground. Strong winds can even roll heavier sediment particles over the ground. Figure 27 shows how wind erodes by deflation.

Deflation does not usually have a great effect on the land. However, in parts of the Great Plains in the 1930s, deflation caused the loss of about 1 meter of topsoil in just a few years. In deserts, deflation can sometimes create an area of rock fragments called desert pavement. You can see an area of desert pavement in Figure 28. There, wind has blown away the smaller sediment. All that remains are rocky materials that are too large and heavy to be moved. Where there is already a slight depression in the ground, deflation can produce a bowl-shaped hollow called a blowout.

Abrasion by wind-carried sand can polish rock, but it causes little erosion. At one time, geologists thought that the sediment carried by wind cut the stone shapes seen in deserts. But now evidence shows that most desert landforms are the result of weathering and water erosion.

Figure 28 Wind erosion formed this desert pavement in the Arizona desert. Wind-driven sand may polish and shape individual stones.

✓ *Checkpoint* *Where would you be most likely to see evidence of wind erosion?*

Figure 29 Wind carrying fine particles of silt built up this loess deposit near Natchez, Mississippi.

Deposits Resulting From Wind Erosion

All the sediment picked up by wind eventually falls to the ground. This happens when the wind slows down or some obstacle, such as a boulder or a clump of grass, traps the windblown sand and other sediment. **Wind erosion and deposition may form sand dunes and loess deposits.** When the wind strikes an obstacle, the result is usually a sand dune. Sand dunes can be seen on beaches and in deserts where wind-blown sediment has built up.

Sand dunes come in many shapes and sizes. Some are long, with parallel ridges, while others are U-shaped. They can also be very small or very large—some sand dunes in China have grown to heights of 500 meters. Sand dunes move over time. Little by little, the sand shifts with the wind from one side of the dune to the other. Sometimes plants begin growing on a dune. Plant roots can help to anchor the dune in one place.

Sand dunes are most often made of the coarser sediments carried by wind. The finer sediments, including particles of clay and silt, are sometimes deposited in layers far from their source. This fine, wind-deposited sediment is **loess** (LES). Large loess deposits are found in central China and in such states as Nebraska, South Dakota, Iowa, Missouri, and Illinois. Loess helps to form fertile soil. Many areas with thick loess deposits are valuable farmlands.

Section 6 Review

Science at Home

1. Describe how wind erodes the land.
2. How do sand dunes and loess deposits form?
3. What is a blowout and what is the process that produces one?
4. **Thinking Critically Predicting** You visit a beach that has sand dunes covered with dune grass. But where people take a shortcut over one dune, the grass has been worn away. What may eventually happen to the dune if people keep taking this path?

Here's how to make a model of desert pavement. Put a few coins in a shallow pan about 1 centimeter deep. Sprinkle enough flour over the coins to bury them beneath a thin layer of flour. Then blow air gently through a straw across the surface of the flour. Be careful not to draw in any flour through the straw. Be certain the blown flour will not get in your or anyone else's eyes. Ask your family to predict what the surface of the pan would look like if the "wind" continued to blow for a long time.

SECTION 1 Changing Earth's Surface

Key Ideas

◆ Weathering, erosion, and deposition act to wear down and build up Earth's surface.

◆ Gravity pulls sediment downhill in the process of mass movement. There are four main types of mass movement: landslides, mudslides, slump, and creep.

Key Terms

erosion   deposition
sediment   mass movement

SECTION 2 Water Erosion

Key Ideas

◆ Moving water is the major force of erosion that has shaped Earth's land surface.

◆ A river may form V-shaped valleys, waterfalls, meanders, oxbow lakes, and flood plains.

◆ When a river slows down, it deposits some of the sediment load it carries, forming features such as alluvial fans and deltas.

Key Terms

runoff	drainage basin	delta
rill	divide	groundwater
gully	flood plain	stalactite
stream	meander	stalagmite
river	oxbow lake	karst topography
tributary	alluvial fan	

SECTION 3 The Force of Moving Water

INTEGRATING PHYSICS

Key Ideas

◆ When gravity pulls water down a slope, water's potential energy changes to kinetic energy, and it does work.

◆ Most sediment washes or falls into streams, or is eroded from the streambed by abrasion.

◆ The greater a river's slope or volume of flow, the more sediment it can erode.

Key Terms

energy	abrasion	friction
potential energy	load	turbulence
kinetic energy		

SECTION 4 Glaciers

Key Ideas

◆ The two kinds of glaciers are valley glaciers and continental glaciers.

◆ Glaciers erode the land through plucking and abrasion. Melting glaciers deposit sediment.

Key Terms

glacier	ice age	moraine
valley glacier	plucking	kettle
continental glacier	till	

SECTION 5 Waves

Key Ideas

◆ The energy of ocean waves comes from wind blowing across the water's surface and transferring energy to the water.

◆ Ocean waves hitting land cause erosion through impact and abrasion. Waves also move and deposit sediment along the shore.

Key Terms

beach   longshore drift   spit

SECTION 6 Wind Erosion

Key Ideas

◆ Wind causes erosion mainly through deflation, the blowing of surface materials.

◆ Landforms created by wind deposition include sand dunes and loess deposits.

Key Terms

sand dune   deflation   loess

Organizing Information

Flowchart Make a flowchart showing how a stream forms. Your flowchart should include the following terms in the correct order: rills, runoff, gullies, stream, raindrops. Give your flowchart a title. (For tips on making a flowchart, see the Skills Handbook.)

Reviewing Content

 For more review of key concepts, see the Interactive Student Tutorial CD-ROM.

Multiple Choice

Choose the answer that best completes the sentence.

1. The eroded materials carried by water or wind are called
   a. stalactites.
   b. desert pavement.
   c. sediment.
   d. moraines.

2. The downhill movement of eroded materials is known as
   a. mass movement.
   b. abrasion.
   c. deposition.
   d. deflation.

3. A mass of rock and soil deposited directly by a glacier is called
   a. load.   b. till.
   c. loess.   d. erosion.

4. When waves strike a shoreline, they concentrate their energy on
   a. beaches.
   b. cirques.
   c. sand dunes.
   d. headlands.

5. The erosion of sediment by wind is
   a. deposition.   b. deflation.
   c. plucking.   d. glaciation.

True or False

If the statement is true, write true. If it is false, change the underlined word or words to make the statement true.

6. The process by which sediment in water settles in new locations is <u>mass movement</u>.

7. An area of <u>alluvial fans</u> may be found where groundwater erodes limestone to form valleys, sinkholes, and caverns.

8. Because it is moving, flowing water has a type of energy called <u>kinetic energy</u>.

9. A looplike bend in the course of a river is a <u>meander</u>.

10. The sediment deposited at the edge of a glacier forms a ridge called a <u>kettle</u>.

Checking Concepts

11. What agents of erosion are in part caused by the force of gravity?

12. How do a river's slope and volume of flow affect the river's sediment load?

13. Describe how the speed of flowing water changes where a river bends. How does this affect a river's deposition of sediment?

14. Why does a delta develop when a river flows into a larger body of water?

15. Describe the process by which groundwater can cause erosion and deposition in limestone beneath Earth's surface.

16. What are ice ages?

17. **Writing to Learn** You go on a rafting journey that takes you down a river from the mountains to the sea. Write a letter to a friend describing the features created by erosion and deposition that you see as you travel down the river. Include features near the river's source, along the middle of its course, and where it reaches the ocean.

Thinking Critically

18. **Applying Concepts** Under what conditions would you expect abrasion to cause the most erosion of a riverbed?

19. **Relating Cause and Effect** In a desert, you see an area that looks as if it were paved with rock fragments. Explain how this situation occurred naturally.

20. **Problem Solving** Suppose you are a geologist studying a valley glacier. What method could you use to tell if it is advancing or retreating?

21. **Making Judgments** A salesperson offers to sell your family a new house right on a riverbank for very little money. Why might your family hesitate to buy this house?

22. **Inferring** You see a sandy beach along a coastline. What can you infer about where the sand came from?

23. **Comparing and Contrasting** How are landslides similar to mudflows? How are they different?

Applying Skills

The table below shows how a river's volume of flow and sediment load change over six months. Use the table to answer Questions 24–26.

Month	Volume of Flow (cubic meters/second)	Sediment Load (metric tons/day)
January	1.5	200
February	1.7	320
March	2.6	725
April	4.0	1600
May	3.2	1100
June	2.8	900

24. **Graphing** Make one graph with the month on the *x*-axis and the volume of flow on the *y*-axis. Make a second graph with the sediment load on the *y*-axis. Compare your two graphs. When were the river's volume of flow and load the greatest? The lowest?

25. **Developing Hypotheses** Use your graphs to develop a hypothesis about the relationship between volume of flow and sediment load.

26. **Relating Cause and Effect** What may have occurred in the river's drainage basin in April to cause the changes in volume of flow and sediment load? Explain.

Performance ▼ CHAPTER PROJECT 3 Assessment

Project Wrap Up Now you are ready to explain your models of erosion to your class. Label your models to indicate the features that changed during erosion.

Reflect and Record In your journal, write about the easiest and hardest parts of this project. How would you do each model differently if you did the project again?

Test Preparation

Use these questions to prepare for standardized tests.

Read the passage. Then answer Questions 27–30.

This is the story of a great river. The Missouri River is America's second longest river after the Mississippi River. Its vast drainage basin covers parts of 10 states and 2 Canadian provinces. Early settlers called the Missouri the "Big Muddy" because its waters carry a heavy sediment load.

The Missouri River begins in the Rocky Mountains near Three Forks, Montana, where three small streams join. The upper Missouri flows through a deep valley called the Gates of the Mountains. Then at Great Falls, Montana, it plunges down a series of waterfalls and rapids.

Leaving the mountains, the middle Missouri flows across the Great Plains. Major tributaries, such as the Yellowstone and Platte rivers, flow into it. The Missouri has eroded a wide valley as it winds through the plains. Steep ridges called bluffs sometimes form the edges of the valley.

The Missouri ends just north of St. Louis, Missouri, where it flows into the Mississippi.

27. A good title for this passage is
   a. The Rivers of America.
   b. Following the Missouri River.
   c. Tributaries of the Missouri River.
   d. Sedimental Journey.

28. A deep valley, waterfalls, and rapids can be found
   a. where the Missouri crosses the Plains.
   b. nowhere along the Missouri.
   c. on the upper Missouri.
   d. on the lower Missouri.

29. Along the middle Missouri's valley are features called
   a. gullies.   b. drainage basins.
   c. gates.   d. bluffs.

30. The nickname "Big Muddy" refers to the Missouri's
   a. sediment load.
   b. source.
   c. meanders.
   d. tributaries.

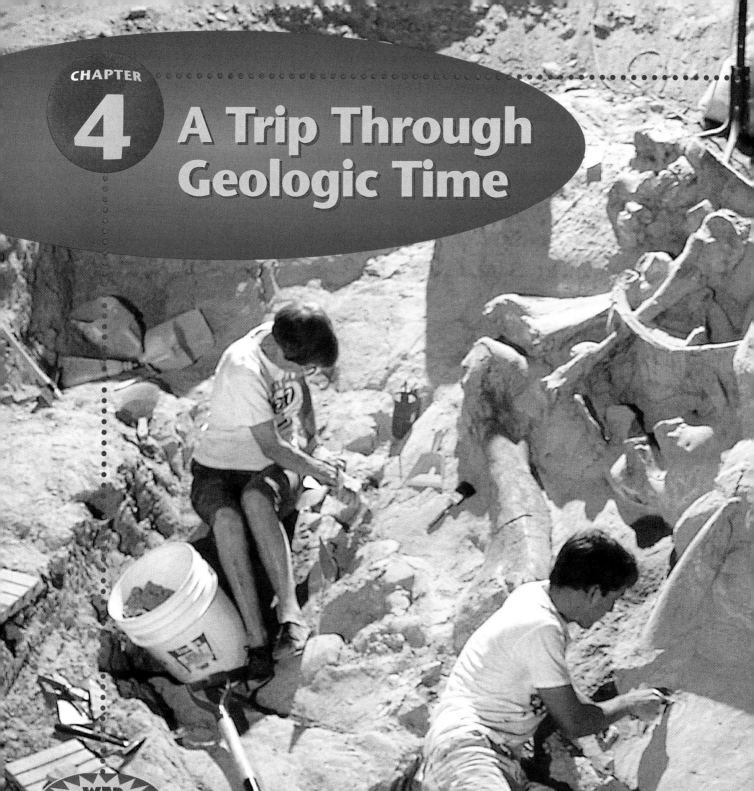

WEB
ACTIVITY www.phschool.com

PROJECT 4

A Journey Back in Time

With great care, scientists remove soil covering the bones of a mammoth. At this site, they have unearthed fossils of more than 30 other animals. These animals lived on the Great Plains during the last Ice Age. From such fossils, scientists can develop a picture of life in the distant past.

This chapter will take you back on a journey through geologic time. You will learn how fossils reveal the history of life on Earth. To guide you on your journey, you and your classmates will make a time line showing the many periods of geologic time.

Your Goal To become an expert on one geologic time period and assist in constructing a time line.

To complete this project, you must
- ◆ research a geologic time period of your choice
- ◆ create a travel brochure that shows what life was like in this time period
- ◆ illustrate your time period for the time line

Get Started Begin by previewing *Exploring Geologic History* on pages 132–135. Select a time period you would like to investigate. Check with your teacher to be sure that all the time periods will be covered by members of your class.

Check Your Progress You will be working on this project as you study this chapter. To keep your project on track, look for Check Your Progress boxes at the following points.

Section 2 Review, page 117: Collect information on the animals, plants, and environment of your time period.

Section 4 Review, page 125: Write a travel brochure about the animals, plants, and environment of your selected time period.

Section 5 Review, page 140: Create illustrations that depict your time period and complete your travel brochure.

Wrap Up At the end of the chapter (page 143), place your illustrations on the time line. Use the travel brochure to present your geologic time period to your classmates.

At a site in South Dakota, scientists uncover mammoth bones that are 26,000 years old. Mammoths were relatives of modern elephants.

 SECTION **4** The Geologic Time Scale

Discover This Is Your Life!
Skills Lab As Time Goes By

 SECTION **5** Earth's History

Discover What Do Fossils Reveal About Earth's History?
Try This Life and Times

SECTION 1 Fossils

DISCOVER

What's in a Rock?

1. Use a hand lens to carefully observe the rock sample provided by your teacher.

2. Make a drawing of any shapes you see in the rock. Include as many details as you can. Beneath your drawing, write a short description of what you see.

Think It Over

Inferring What do you think the rock contains? How do you think the shapes you observed in the rock got there?

GUIDE FOR READING

◆ How do fossils form?

◆ What are the different kinds of fossils?

◆ What do fossils tell about how organisms have changed over time?

Reading Tip As you read, use the headings to make an outline showing what fossils are, how they form, and why they are important.

You are a geologist at work in the high mountains of western Canada. You carefully split apart a piece of soft rock. Pressed into the rock is the shape of a tiny animal about the size of your thumb. The animal looks like no creature you have ever seen.

The rock is from a layer of rocks called the Burgess shale. The Burgess shale is famous because it contains evidence of life on Earth more than 500 million years ago. The creatures in the Burgess shale are tiny, soft-bodied animals without backbones. Some look like present-day crabs or worms. These animals lived on the bottom of a shallow sea. Scientists hypothesize that a mudslide suddenly buried the animals. Over millions of years, the mud turned to shale. The remains of the animals also became solid rock.

Evidence of Ancient Life

Fossils are the preserved remains or traces of living things. Fossils provide evidence of how life has changed over time. Fossils also help scientists infer how Earth's surface has changed. Fossils are clues to what past environments were like.

Most fossils form when living things die and are buried by sediments. The sediments slowly harden into rock and preserve the shapes of the organisms. Scientists who study fossils are called **paleontologists** (pay lee un TAHL uh jists). Fossils are usually found in sedimentary rock.

Figure 1 Paleontologists chip out the fossil-bearing rock of the Burgess shale.

Figure 2 A fossil may form when sediment quickly covers an animal's body. *Predicting What would happen to the fossil if erosion continued after Step D?*

A. An animal dies and sinks into shallow water.

B. Sediment covers the animal.

C. The sediment becomes rock, preserving parts of the animal.

D. Mountain building, weathering, and erosion eventually expose the fossil at the surface.

Sedimentary rock is the type of rock that is made of hardened sediment. Most fossils form from animals or plants that once lived in or near quiet water such as swamps, lakes, or shallow seas where sediments build up. In Figure 2, you can see how a fossil might form.

When an organism dies, its soft parts often decay quickly or are eaten by animals. Thus, generally only hard parts leave fossils. These hard parts include bones, shells, teeth, seeds, and woody stems. It is rare for the soft parts of an organism to become a fossil.

Figure 3 Although they look as if they were just cut down, these petrified tree trunks were formed 200 million years ago. These fossils can be seen in the Petrified Forest National Park in Arizona.

Kinds of Fossils

For a fossil to form, the remains or traces of an organism must be protected from decay. Then one of several processes may cause a fossil to form. **Fossils found in rock include petrified fossils, molds and casts, carbon films, and trace fossils. Other fossils form when the remains of organisms are preserved in substances such as tar, amber, or ice.**

Petrified Fossils A fossil may form when the remains of an organism become petrified. The term *petrified* means "turning into stone." **Petrified fossils** are fossils in which minerals replace all or part of an organism. The fossil tree trunks shown in Figure 3 are examples of petrified wood. These fossils formed after sediment covered the wood. Then water rich in dissolved minerals seeped into spaces in the plant's cells. Over time, the water evaporated, leaving the hardened minerals behind. Some of the original wood remains, but the minerals have hardened and preserved it.

Sweet Fossils

ACTIVITY

1. Wrap a piece of clay around one sugar cube so that half of it is covered with clay.

2. Wrap clay entirely around a second sugar cube and seal it tightly.

3. Drop both cubes into a bowl of water, along with an uncovered sugar cube.

4. Stir until the uncovered sugar cube dissolves completely.

5. Remove the other cubes from the water and examine the remains.

Observing Describe the appearance of the two sugar cubes. Did the clay preserve the sugar cubes? How does this activity model the way fossils form?

Petrified fossils may also form by replacement. In replacement, the minerals in water make a copy of the organism. For example, water containing dissolved minerals may slowly dissolve a clamshell buried in sediment. At the same time, the minerals in the water harden to form rock. The result is a copy of the clamshell made of rock.

Molds and Casts The most common fossils are molds and casts. Both copy the shape of ancient organisms. A **mold** is a hollow area in sediment in the shape of an organism or part of an organism. A mold forms when the hard part of the organism, such as a shell, is buried in sediment.

Later, water carrying dissolved minerals and sediment may seep into the empty space of a mold. If the water deposits the minerals and sediment there, the result is a cast. A **cast** is a copy of the shape of an organism. Figure 4 shows a mold (top) that became filled with minerals to form a cast (bottom). As you can see, a cast is the opposite of its mold. Also notice how the mold and cast have preserved details of the animal's structure.

Figure 4 The fossil mold (top) clearly shows the shape of the animal called *Cryptolithus.* So does the fossil cast (bottom). *Cryptolithus* lived in the oceans about 450 million years ago.

Carbon Films Another type of fossil is a **carbon film,** an extremely thin coating of carbon on rock. How does a carbon film form? Remember that all living things contain carbon. When sediment buries an organism, some of the materials that make up the organism evaporate or become gases. These gases escape from the sediment, leaving carbon behind. Eventually, only a thin film of carbon remains. This process can preserve the delicate parts of plant leaves and insects.

INTEGRATING CHEMISTRY

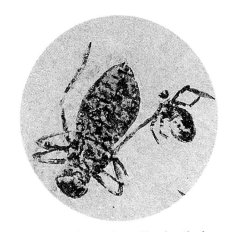

Figure 5 This carbon film fossil of insects is between 5 million and 23 million years old.

Trace Fossils Most types of fossils preserve the shapes of ancient animals and plants. In contrast, **trace fossils** provide evidence of the activities of ancient organisms. A fossilized footprint is one example of a trace fossil. A dinosaur made the fossil footprint shown in Figure 6. The mud or sand that the animal stepped into eventually was buried by layers of sediment. Slowly the sediment became solid rock, preserving the footprints for millions of years.

Fossil footprints provide clues about an animal's size and behavior. How fast could the animal move? Did it walk on two or four legs? Did it live alone or with others of its kind? A scientist can infer the answers to such questions by looking at fossil footprints.

Other examples of trace fossils include the trails that animals followed or the burrows that they lived in. A trail or burrow can give clues about the size and shape of the organism, where it lived, and how it obtained food.

✓ *Checkpoint* *What can a trace fossil reveal about an early animal?*

Preserved Remains Some processes preserve the remains of organisms with little or no change. For example, some remains are preserved when organisms become trapped in tar. Tar is sticky oil that seeps from Earth's surface. Many fossils preserved in tar have been found at the Rancho La Brea tar pits in Los Angeles, California. Thousands of years ago, animals came to drink the water that covered these pits. Somehow, they became stuck in the tar

Figure 6 These dinosaur footprints are in the Painted Desert in Arizona. *Inferring What can you infer about this dinosaur from its footprints?*

Figure 7 A fossil preserved in amber provides a window into the history of past life on Earth. Body parts, including the hairlike bristles on an insect's legs, its antennae, and its delicate wings, are often perfectly preserved.

and then died. The tar soaked into their bones, preserving the bones from decay.

Ancient organisms also have been preserved in amber. Amber is the hardened resin, or sap, of evergreen trees. First, an insect is trapped on sticky resin. After the insect dies, more resin covers it, sealing it from air and protecting its body from decay.

Freezing is another way in which remains can be preserved. The frozen remains of relatives of elephants called woolly mammoths have been found in very cold regions of Siberia and Alaska. Freezing has preserved even the mammoths' hair and skin.

☑ *Checkpoint* *What are three ways in which the remains of an organism can be preserved?*

Change Over Time

Paleontologists collect fossils from sedimentary rocks all over the world. They use this information to determine what past life forms were like. They want to learn what these organisms ate, what ate them, and in what environment they lived.

Paleontologists also classify organisms. They group similar organisms together. They arrange organisms in the order in which they lived, from earliest to latest. Together, all the information that paleontologists have gathered about past life is called the fossil record. **The fossil record provides evidence about the history of life on Earth. The fossil record also shows that different groups of organisms have changed over time.**

The fossil record reveals a surprising fact: Fossils occur in a particular order. Older rocks contain fossils of simpler organisms. Younger rocks contain fossils of more complex organisms. In other words, the fossil record shows that life on Earth has evolved, or changed. Simple, one-celled organisms have given rise to complex plants and animals.

The fossil record provides evidence to support the theory of evolution. A **scientific theory** is a well-tested concept that explains a wide range of observations. **Evolution** is the gradual change in living things over long periods of time. You can trace the evolution of one group of animals in *Exploring the Evolution of Elephants.*

The fossil record shows that millions of types of organisms have evolved. But many others have become extinct. A type of organism is **extinct** if it no longer exists and will never again live on Earth.

EXPLORING the Evolution of Elephants

Here are some members of the elephant family. Modern elephants, mammoths, and mastodons all evolved from a common ancestor that lived about 34 million years ago.

**Asian Elephant
present day**
Asian elephants live in India and Southeast Asia. They can be trained to move objects with their trunks and to carry heavy loads on their backs.

**African Elephant
present day**
About 4 meters high at the shoulder, the African elephant is larger than the Asian elephant. African elephants are fierce and difficult to tame.

**Woolly Mammoth
2 million years ago**
The woolly mammoth lived during the last Ice Age. Hunting by humans may have led to their extinction about 10,000 years ago.

**Mastodon
25–30 million years ago**
Mastodons developed long, flexible trunks and long tusks. Later mastodons looked similar to mammoths, but were smaller and stockier. Mastodons became extinct about 10,000 years ago.

Gomphotherium
23 million years ago
Gomphotherium stood over 2 meters at the shoulder. It had a small trunk, two tusks on the upper jaw, and two tusks on the lower jaw.

Moeritherium
36 million years ago
A pig-sized relative of modern elephants, *Moeritherium* had long front teeth—primitive tusks—and a long upper lip.

**Paleomastodon
34 million years ago**
Paleomastodons had a short trunk and short tusks on both upper and lower jaws. The paleomastodon was an ancestor of later elephantlike animals.

Figure 8 These are fossils of brachiopods and crinoids that lived more than 435 million years ago. Similar organisms still live in the oceans today. From these fossils, scientists know that the environment where they were found was once a shallow sea.

Fossils and Past Environments

Paleontologists use fossils to build up a picture of Earth's environments in the past. The fossils found in an area tell whether the area was a shallow bay, an ocean bottom, or a fresh-water swamp.

Fossils also provide evidence of Earth's climate in the past. For example, coal has been found in Antarctica. But coal only forms from the remains of plants that grow in warm, swampy regions. As you probably know, thick layers of ice and snow now cover Antarctica. The presence of coal shows that the climate of Antarctica was once much warmer than it is today.

Scientists can use fossils to learn about changes in Earth's surface. For example, corals are organisms that thrive in warm, shallow seas. Yet fossil corals are often found in many areas of the midwestern United States. From this fact, scientists infer that shallow seas once covered those areas.

Section 1 Review

1. Describe the process by which most fossils are formed in rock.
2. What are the five types of fossils that can be found in rock?
3. How does the fossil record support the theory of evolution?
4. Describe one way in which the remains of an organism can be preserved.
5. **Thinking Critically Inferring** Fossil seashells have been found in rock beds on land. What can you infer about how the area has changed?

Science at Home

A fossil is something old that has been preserved. Why is it that some old things are preserved, while others are destroyed? With your parents' permission, look around your house for the oldest object you can find. Interview family members to determine how old the object is, why it has been preserved, and how it may have changed since it was new. Make a drawing of the object and bring it to class. Tell your class the story of this "fossil."

SECTION 2 Finding the Relative Age of Rocks

Have you ever seen rock layers exposed on a cliff beside a road? Often the rock layers differ in color or texture. What are these layers, and how did they form?

The sediment that forms sedimentary rocks is deposited in flat layers one on top of the other. Over years, the sediment becomes deeply buried. Then it hardens and changes into sedimentary rock. At the same time, remains of organisms in the sediment may become fossils. Over time, many layers of sediment become different layers of rock. These rock layers provide a record of Earth's geologic history.

Relative and Absolute Ages

When you look at a rock containing a fossil, your first question may be, "How old is it?" The **relative age** of a rock is its age compared to the ages of other rocks. You have probably used the idea of relative age when comparing your age with someone else's age. For example, if you say that you are older than your brother but younger than your sister, you are describing your relative age.

The relative age of a rock does not provide its absolute age. The **absolute age** of a rock is the number of years since the rock formed. It may be impossible to know a rock's absolute age exactly. But sometimes geologists can determine a rock's absolute age to within a certain number of years.

GUIDE FOR READING

◆ How do geologists determine the relative age of rocks?

◆ How are index fossils useful to geologists?

Reading Tip Before you read, rewrite the headings in the section as *how, why,* or *what* questions. As you read, look for answers to these questions.

Kaibab limestone
250 million years old

Toroweap limestone
255 million years old

Coconino sandstone
260 million years old

Hermit shale
265 million years old

Supai sandstone
285 million years old

Younger

Older

Figure 9 More than a dozen rock layers make up the walls of the Grand Canyon. You can see five layers clearly in the photograph. *Applying Concepts In which of the labeled layers in the diagram would you find the oldest fossils? Explain.*

Sampling a Sandwich

Your teacher will give you a sandwich that represents rock layers in Earth's crust.

1. Use a round, hollow, uncooked noodle as a coring tool. Push the noodle through the layers of the sandwich.

2. Pull the noodle out of the sandwich. Break the noodle gently to remove your core sample.

3. Draw a picture coloring and labeling what you see in each layer of the core.

Observing If this were a real sample of rock layers, which layer would be the oldest? The youngest? Why do you think scientists study core samples?

The Position of Rock Layers

It can be difficult to determine the absolute age of a rock. So geologists use a method to find a rock's relative age. Geologists use the **law of superposition** to determine the relative ages of sedimentary rock layers. **According to the law of superposition, in horizontal sedimentary rock layers the oldest layer is at the bottom. Each higher layer is younger than the layers below it.** If you did the Discover activity at the beginning of this section, you have already used the law of superposition.

The walls of the Grand Canyon in Arizona illustrate the law of superposition. The sedimentary rock layers in the canyon walls represent 2 billion years of Earth's history. You can see some of the rock layers found in the Grand Canyon in Figure 9. Scientists have given names to all the layers of rock exposed on the walls of the Grand Canyon. By using the law of superposition, you should be able to determine the relative ages of these layers.

If you were to start at the top of the Grand Canyon, you would see Kaibab limestone. Because it is on top, it is the youngest layer. As you began your descent into the canyon, you would pass by Toroweap limestone. Next, you would see Coconino sandstone. The deeper you traveled into the canyon, the older the rocks would become. Your trip into the canyon is like a trip into Earth's history. The deeper you go, the older the rocks.

✓ *Checkpoint* How would a geologist find the relative age of a rock?

Other Clues to Relative Age

There are other clues to the relative ages of rocks. Geologists find some of these clues by studying extrusions and intrusions of igneous rock and faults.

Clues From Igneous Rock Igneous rock forms when magma or lava hardens. Magma is molten material beneath Earth's surface. Magma that flows onto the surface is called lava.

Lava that hardens on the surface is called an **extrusion.** The rock layers below an extrusion are always older than the extrusion.

Beneath the surface, magma may push into bodies of rock. There, the magma cools and hardens into a mass of igneous rock called an **intrusion.** An intrusion is always younger than the rock layers around and beneath it. Figure 10A shows an intrusion. Geologists study where intrusions and extrusions formed in relation to other rock layers. This helps geologists understand the relative ages of the different types of rock.

Clues From Faults More clues come from the study of faults. A **fault** is a break in Earth's crust. Forces inside Earth cause movement of the rock on opposite sides of a fault.

A fault is always younger than the rock it cuts through. To determine the relative age of a fault, geologists find the the relative age of the most recent rock layer through which the fault slices.

Movements along faults can make it harder for geologists to determine the relative ages of rock layers. In Figure 10B you can see how the rock layers no longer line up because of movement along the fault.

Music CONNECTION

The Grand Canyon provides one of Earth's best views of the geologic record. The American composer Ferde Grofé composed his *Grand Canyon Suite* for orchestra in 1931. The music paints a picture of desert scenery and a trip on muleback into the Grand Canyon.

In Your Journal

Listen to a recording of the *Grand Canyon Suite.* How does Grofé's music express what it's like to visit the Grand Canyon? What words would you use to describe what you heard?

Figure 10 Intrusions and faults give clues to the relative ages of rocks. In 10A, an intrusion cuts through rock layers. In 10B, rock layers are broken and shifted along a fault. *Inferring Which is older, the intrusion in 10A or the rock layers it crosses?*

1. Sedimentary rocks form in horizontal layers.

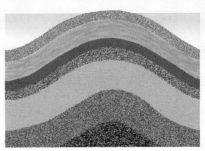

2. Folding tilts the rock layers.

Figure 11 An unconformity occurs where erosion wears away layers of sedimentary rock. Other rock layers then form on top of the eroded surface.

3. The surface is eroded.

Unconformity

4. New sediment is deposited, forming rock layers above the unconformity.

Gaps in the Geologic Record

The geologic record of sedimentary rock layers is not always complete. Deposition slowly builds layer upon layer of sedimentary rock. But some of these layers may erode away, exposing an older rock surface. Then deposition begins again, building new rock layers.

The surface where new rock layers meet a much older rock surface beneath them is called an unconformity. An **unconformity** is a gap in the geologic record. An unconformity shows where some rock layers have been lost because of erosion. Figure 11 shows how an unconformity forms.

Using Fossils to Date Rocks

Figure 12 Trilobite fossils are widely distributed. Some types of trilobites serve as index fossils.

To date rock layers, geologists first give a relative age to a layer of rock at one location. Then they can give the same age to matching layers of rock at other locations.

Certain fossils, called index fossils, help geologists match rock layers. To be useful as an **index fossil,** a fossil must be widely distributed and represent a type of organism that existed only briefly. A fossil is considered widely distributed if it occurs in many different areas. Geologists look for index fossils in layers of rock. **Index fossils are useful because they tell the relative ages of the rock layers in which they occur.**

Geologists use particular types of organisms as index fossils—for example, certain types of trilobites. Trilobites (TRY luh byts) were a group of hard-shelled animals whose bodies had three

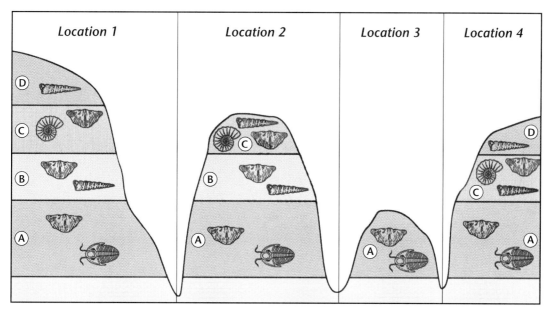

| Location 1 | Location 2 | Location 3 | Location 4 |

Figure 13 Scientists use index fossils to match up rock layers at locations that may be far apart. The trilobites in Layer A are index fossils. *Interpreting Diagrams Can you find another index fossil in the diagram?* (*Hint:* Look for a fossil that occurs in only one time period, but in several different locations.)

distinct parts. Trilobites evolved in shallow seas more than 500 million years ago. Over time, many different types of trilobites appeared. They became extinct about 245 million years ago. Trilobite fossils have been found in many different places.

To serve as an index fossil, a type of trilobite must be different in some way from other trilobites. One example is a type of trilobite with large eyes. These large-eyed trilobites survived for a time after other trilobites became extinct. Suppose a geologist finds large-eyed trilobites in a rock layer. The geologist can infer that those rocks are younger than rocks containing other types of trilobites.

You can use index fossils to match rock layers. Look at Figure 13, which shows rock layers from four different locations. Notice that two of the fossils are found in only one of these rock layers. These are the index fossils.

 Section 2 Review

1. What is the law of superposition?
2. What characteristics are necessary for a fossil to be considered an index fossil?
3. What do unconformities show?
4. **Thinking Critically Applying Concepts** Horseshoe crabs are common in the ocean along the east coast of North America. They have existed with very little change for about 200 million years. Would horseshoe crabs be useful as an index fossil? Explain why or why not.

Check Your Progress
CHAPTER PROJECT 4
Locate reference materials you will need to research your chosen geologic time period. Possible sources include library books, magazines, encyclopedias, and Internet articles. Also keep a list of the resources you used. As you do your research, keep in mind the pictures and facts you will need for the class time line and travel brochure. Be sure to include the organisms and environment of the time period.

You Be the Detective

Finding Clues to ROCK-LAYERS

Fossil clues give geologists a good idea of what life on Earth was like millions or even billions of years ago.

Problem

How can you use fossils and geologic features to interpret the relative ages of rock layers?

Skills Focus

interpreting data, drawing conclusions

Procedure

1. Study the rock layers at Sites 1 and 2. Write down the similarities and differences between the layers at the two sites.
2. List the kinds of fossils that are found in each rock layer of Sites 1 and 2.

Analyze and Conclude

Site 1

1. What "fossil clues" in layers A and B indicate the kind of environment that existed when these rock layers were formed? How did the environment change in layer D?
2. Which layer is the oldest? How do you know?

3. Which of the layers formed most recently? How do you know?
4. Why are there no fossils in layers C and E?
5. What kind of fossils occurred in layer F?

Site 2

6. Which layer at Site 1 might have formed at the same time as layer W at Site 2?
7. What clues show an unconformity or gap in the horizontal rock layers? Which rock layers are missing? What might have happened to these rock layers?
8. Which is older, intrusion V or layer Y? How do you know?
9. **Think About It** Working as a geologist, you find a rock containing fossils. What information would you need in order to determine this rock's age relative to one of the rock layers at Site 1?

More to Explore

Draw a sketch similar to Site 2 and include a fault that cuts across the intrusion. Have a partner then identify the relative age of the fault, the intrusion, and the layers cut by the fault.

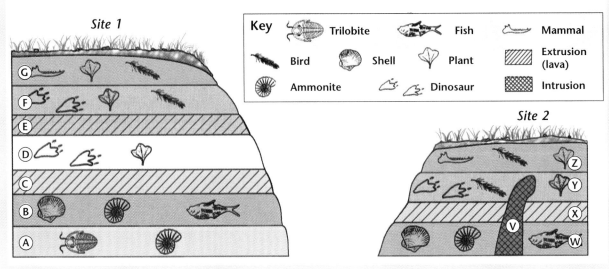

Site 1

Key Trilobite Fish Mammal
Bird Shell Plant Extrusion (lava)
Ammonite Dinosaur Intrusion

Site 2

SECTION 3 Radioactive Dating

In Australia, scientists have found sedimentary rocks that contain some of the world's oldest fossils—stromatolites (stroh MAT uh lyts). Stromatolites are the remains of reefs built by organisms similar to present-day bacteria. The bacteria grew together in dense mats shaped like stacks of pancakes. The mats formed reefs in shallow water near the shores of ancient oceans. Sediment eventually covered these reefs. As the sediments changed to rock, so did the reefs.

Paleontologists have determined that some stromatolites are more than 3 billion years old. But how did scientists determine the age of these fossils? To understand the methods of absolute dating, you need to learn more about the chemistry of rocks.

Changing From One Element to Another

What do you, the air you breathe, a lemon, and a puddle of water have in common? All are kinds of matter. In fact, everything around you is made of matter. Although different kinds of matter look, feel, or smell different, all the matter you see is made of tiny particles called **atoms.** When all the atoms in a particular type of matter are the same, the matter is an **element.** Carbon, oxygen, iron, lead, and potassium are just some of the more than 110 currently known elements.

Figure 14 Stromatolites were formed by clumps of one-celled organisms that lived in shallow seas more than 3 billion years ago. Similar organisms grow in the ocean near Australia today.

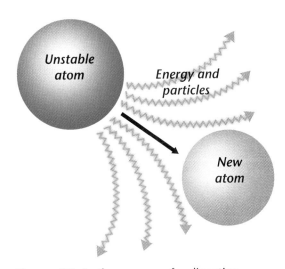

Figure 15 In the process of radioactive decay, an atom releases energy.

Most elements are stable. They do not change under normal conditions. But some elements exist in forms that are unstable. Over time, these elements break down, or decay, by releasing particles and energy in a process called **radioactive decay.** These unstable elements are said to be radioactive. **During radioactive decay, the atoms of one element break down to form atoms of another element.** Radioactive elements occur naturally in igneous rocks. Scientists use the rate at which these elements decay to calculate the rock's age.

The Rate of Radioactive Decay

You have a birthday, a specific day from which you calculate your age. What's the "birthday" of a rock? For an igneous rock, that "birthday" is when it first hardens to become rock. (Recall that igneous rocks form from molten magma and lava.) As a radioactive element within the igneous rock decays, it changes into another element. So the composition of the rock changes slowly over time. The amount of the radioactive element goes down. But the amount of the new element goes up.

The rate of decay of each radioactive element is constant—it never changes. This rate of decay is the element's half-life. The **half-life** of a radioactive element is the time it takes for half of the radioactive atoms to decay. You can see in Figure 16 how a radioactive element decays over time.

Figure 16 The half-life of a radioactive element is the amount of time it takes for half of the radioactive atoms to decay. *Calculating After three half-lives, how much of the radioactive element remains?*

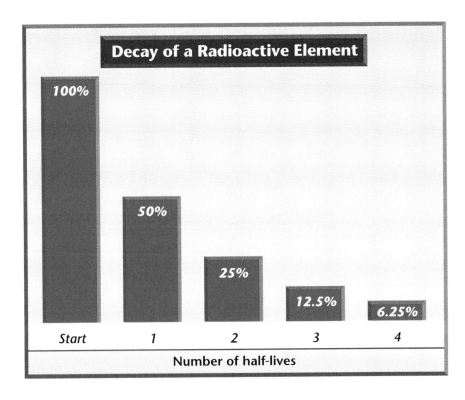

Elements Used in Radioactive Dating		
Radioactive Element	Half-life (years)	Dating Range (years)
Carbon-14	5,730	500–50,000
Potassium-40	1.3 billion	50,000–4.6 billion
Rubidium-87	47 billion	10 million–4.6 billion
Thorium-232	14.1 billion	10 million–4.6 billion
Uranium-235	713 million	10 million–4.6 billion
Uranium-238	4.5 billion	10 million–4.6 billion

Figure 17 The half-lives of different radioactive elements vary greatly. This scientist is testing a sample of material to determine how much carbon-14 it contains.

Absolute Ages From Radioactive Dating

Geologists use radioactive dating to determine the absolute ages of rocks. In radioactive dating, scientists first determine the amount of a radioactive element in a rock. Then they compare that amount with the amount of the stable element into which the radioactive element decays. Figure 17 lists several common radioactive elements and their half-lives.

Potassium–Argon Dating Scientists often date rocks using potassium-40. This form of potassium decays to stable argon-40 and has a half-life of 1.3 billion years. Potassium-40 is useful in dating the most ancient rocks because of its long half-life.

Carbon-14 Dating A radioactive form of carbon is carbon-14. All plants and animals contain carbon, including some carbon-14. As plants and animals grow, carbon atoms are added to their tissues. After an organism dies, no more carbon is added. But the carbon-14 in the organism's body decays. It changes to stable nitrogen-14. To determine the age of a sample, scientists measure the amount of carbon-14 that is left in the organism's remains. From this amount, they can determine its absolute age. Carbon-14 has been used to date fossils such as frozen mammoths, as well as pieces of wood and bone. Carbon-14 even has been used to date the skeletons of prehistoric humans.

Carbon-14 is very useful in dating materials from plants and animals that lived up to about 50,000 years ago. Carbon-14 has a half-life of only 5,730 years. For this reason, it can't be used to date really ancient fossils or rocks. The amount of carbon-14 left would be too small to measure accurately.

Checkpoint *What are two types of radioactive dating?*

Sharpen your Skills

Calculating ACTIVITY

You have 3 grams of the radioactive element potassium-40. Calculate the mass of the remaining potassium-40 after 4 half-lives. Now calculate how much time has gone by. (*Hint:* One half-life of potassium-40 takes 1.3 billion years.) What would happen to the amount of potassium-40 if you continued through several more half-lives?

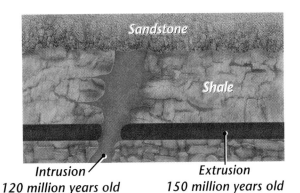

Sandstone

Shale

Intrusion
120 million years old

Extrusion
150 million years old

Figure 18 Radioactive dating has been used to determine the absolute ages of the intrusion and extrusion in the diagram. The shale lies above the extrusion and is crossed by the intrusion. Therefore the shale is younger than the extrusion, but older than the intrusion—between 150 million years old and 120 million years old. *Inferring What can you infer about the age of the sandstone?*

Radioactive Dating of Rock Layers

Radioactive dating cannot usually be used for dating rocks other than igneous rocks. As you recall, sedimentary rocks form as sediments are deposited by water or wind. The rock particles in sedimentary rocks are from other rocks, all of different ages. Radioactive dating would provide the age of the particles. It would not provide the age of the sedimentary rock.

How, then, do scientists date sedimentary rock layers? They date the igneous intrusions and extrusions near the sedimentary rock layers. Look at Figure 18. As you can see, sedimentary rock above an igneous intrusion must be younger than that intrusion.

How Old is Earth?

Radioactive dating has been used to calculate the age of Earth. The oldest rocks ever found on Earth have been dated at about 4.0 billion years old. But scientists think Earth formed even earlier than that. According to one theory, Earth and the moon are about the same age. When Earth was very young, a large object from space collided with Earth. This collision threw a large amount of material from both bodies into orbit around Earth. This material combined to form the moon. Scientists have dated moon rocks brought to Earth by astronauts during the 1970s. **Radioactive dating shows that the oldest moon rocks are about 4.6 billion years old. Scientists infer that Earth is only a little older than those moon rocks—roughly 4.6 billion years old.**

Section 3 Review

1. Describe the process of radioactive decay.
2. What is a half-life? How is it used to determine the absolute age of a rock?
3. When do scientists use both radioactive dating and relative dating to find the age of a rock?
4. How were moon rocks used to determine the age of Earth?
5. **Thinking Critically Applying Concepts** Which of the following types of fossils can be dated using carbon-14: molds and casts, trace fossils, frozen remains, remains preserved in tar? Explain your answer.

Science at Home

Collect 10 items out of a drawer that is full of odds and ends such as keys, coins, receipts, photographs, and souvenirs. Have your family members put them in order from oldest to newest. What clues will you use to determine their relative ages? Do you remember when certain items were bought or a photograph was taken? How can you determine the oldest object of all? Make a list of the ten items in order by relative age. Are there any items for which you know the absolute age?

SECTION 4 The Geologic Time Scale

DISCOVER • ACTIVITY

This Is Your Life!

1. Make a list of about 10 to 15 important events that you remember in your life.

2. On a sheet of paper, draw a time line to represent your life. Use a scale of 3.0 cm to 1 year.

3. Write each event in the correct year along the time line.

4. Now divide the time line into parts that describe major periods in your life, for example: preschool years, elementary school years, and middle school years.

Think It Over

Making Models Along which part of your time line are most of the events located? Which period of your life does this part of the time line represent? Why do you think this is so?

Imagine squeezing Earth's 4.6-billion-year history into a 24-hour day. Earth forms at midnight. About seven hours later, the earliest one-celled organisms appear. Over the next 14 hours, simple, soft-bodied organisms such as jellyfish and worms develop. A little after 9:00 P.M.—21 hours later—larger, more complex organisms evolve in the oceans. Reptiles and insects first appear about an hour after that. Dinosaurs arrive just before 11:00 P.M., but are extinct by 11:30 P.M. Modern humans don't appear until less than a second before midnight!

GUIDE FOR READING

◆ Why is the geologic time scale used to show Earth's history?

◆ What are the different units of the geologic time scale?

Reading Tip As you read, make a list of the units of geologic time scale. Write a sentence about each.

The Geologic Time Scale

Months, years, or even centuries aren't very helpful for thinking about Earth's long history. **Because the time span of Earth's past is so great, geologists use the geologic time scale to show Earth's history.** The **geologic time scale** is a record of the life forms and geologic events in Earth's history. You can see this time scale in Figure 19.

Scientists first developed the geologic time scale by studying rock layers and index fossils worldwide. With this information, scientists placed Earth's rocks in order by relative age. Later, radioactive dating helped determine the absolute age of the divisions in the geologic time scale. As geologists studied the fossil record, they found major changes in life forms at different times. They used these changes to mark where one unit of geologic time ends and the next begins. Therefore the divisions of the geologic time scale depend on events in the history of life on Earth.

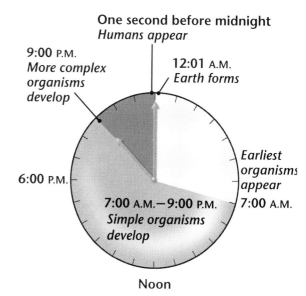

Figure 19 If geologic time went by in a single day, all of human history would take place in less than the last second!

Chapter 4 **G ◆ 123**

Geologic Time Scale

Era	Period	Millions of Years Ago	Duration (millions of years)
Cenozoic	Quaternary	– – – 1.6 – – –	1.6 to present
Cenozoic	Tertiary		65
		– –66.4 – –	
Mesozoic	Cretaceous		78
		– – 144 – –	
Mesozoic	Jurassic		64
		– –208 – – –	
Mesozoic	Triassic		37
		– –245 – –	
Paleozoic	Permian		41
		– –286 – – –	
Paleozoic	Carboniferous		74
		– –360 – –	
Paleozoic	Devonian		48
		– –408 – –	
Paleozoic	Silurian		30
		– –438 – –	
Paleozoic	Ordovician		67
		– –505 – –	
Paleozoic	Cambrian		39
		– –544 – –	
Precambrian			544 million years ago– 4.6 billion years ago

Figure 20 The eras and periods of the geologic time scale are used to date the events in Earth's long history. *Interpreting Diagrams How long ago did the Paleozoic Era end?*

Divisions of Geologic Time

When speaking of the past, what names do you use for different spans of time? You probably use such names as *century, decade, year, month, week,* and *day.* You know that a month is longer than a week but shorter than a year. Scientists use similar divisions for the geologic time scale.

Geologic time begins with a long span of time called Precambrian Time (pree KAM bree un). Precambrian Time, which covers about 88 percent of Earth's history, ended 544 million years ago. **After Precambrian Time, the basic units of the geologic time scale are eras, periods, and epochs.**

☑ *Checkpoint* How much of Earth's history is included in Precambrian Time?

Eras, Periods, and Epochs

Geologists divide the time between Precambrian Time and the present into three long units of time called **eras.** They are the Paleozoic Era, the Mesozoic Era, and the Cenozoic Era.

Eras The Paleozoic (pay lee uh ZOH ik) began about 544 million years ago and lasted for 300 million years. The word part *paleo-* means "ancient or early," and *-zoic* means "life." Many animals that lived during the Paleozoic were animals without backbones, or **invertebrates.**

The Mesozoic (mez uh ZOH ik) began about 245 million years ago and lasted about 180 million years. The word part *meso-* means "middle." People often call the Mesozoic the Age of Dinosaurs. Yet dinosaurs were only one of the many groups of organisms that lived during this era. For example, mammals began to evolve during the Mesozoic Era.

Earth's most recent era is the Cenozoic (sen uh ZOH ik). It began about 65 million years ago and continues to the present day. The word part *ceno-* means "recent." The Cenozoic is sometimes called the Age of Mammals, because mammals became common during this time.

Periods Eras are subdivided into units of geologic time called **periods.** Geologic periods range in length from tens of millions of years to less than two million years. You can see in Figure 20 that the Mesozoic Era includes three periods: the Triassic Period, the Jurassic Period, and the Cretaceous Period.

You may wonder where the names of the geologic periods come from. Many come from places around the world where geologists first described the rocks and fossils of that period. The name Cambrian, for example, refers to Cambria, the old Roman name for Wales. Jurassic refers to the Jura Mountains in France.

The Carboniferous Period is named for the large coal deposits that formed during that period. *Carboniferous* means "carbon bearing." Geologists in the United States often divide the Carboniferous Period into the Mississippian Period (320–360 million years ago) and the Pennsylvanian Period (286–320 million years ago.)

Epochs Geologists further subdivide the periods of the Cenozoic Era into **epochs.** Why are epochs used in the time scale? The fossil record in the Cenozoic is much more complete than the fossil record of earlier eras. There are a lot more events to place in sequence, and using epochs makes this task easier.

Figure 21 The sedimentary rock layers (top) were laid down during the Ordovician period. The fossil of the plant (bottom) formed during the Carboniferous period.

Section 4 Review

1. What is the geologic time scale?
2. What are geologic periods?
3. What method of dating did geologists first use when they developed the geologic time scale? How is the scale different today?
4. **Thinking Critically Interpreting Diagrams** Which period in the Paleozoic was the longest? If you could travel back in time 100 million years, what period would you be in? What era would you be in?

Check Your Progress

CHAPTER PROJECT 4

Make a list of illustrations for the time line and travel brochure. Before creating the illustrations, think about what they will look like and the materials you will need to complete them. Will they be three dimensional? Will they be drawn using a computer? Begin to plan how you will use illustrations in your travel brochure. Space in a brochure is limited, so focus on the highlights of your geologic period.

As Time Goes By

Earth's history goes back 4.6 billion years. How can people grasp the vast scale of geologic time? In this lab, you will make a model to represent Earth's history.

Problem

How can you make a model of geologic time?

Materials

worksheet with 2,000 asterisks
one ream of paper

Procedure

Part 1 Table A

1. Copy Table A into your lab notebook. Figure how long ago these historic events happened and write the answers on your chart.

2. Obtain a worksheet with 2,000 asterisks printed on it. Each asterisk represents one year. The first asterisk at the top represents one year ago.

3. Starting from this asterisk, circle the asterisk that represents how many years ago each event in Table A occurred.

4. Label each circled asterisk to indicate the event.

5. Obtain a ream of copy paper. There are 500 sheets in a ream. If each sheet had 2,000 asterisks on it, there would be a total of 1 million asterisks. Therefore, each ream would represent 1 million years.

Part 2 Fill in Chart B

6. Copy Table B into your lab notebook. Determine how much paper in reams or sheets would be needed to represent the events in geologic time found in Table B. (*Hint:* Recall that each ream represents 1 million years.)

Table A Historic Events		
Event	**Date**	**Number of Years Ago**
You are born		
One of your parents is born		
Space shuttle *Challenger* explodes	1986	
Neil Armstrong first walks on the moon	1969	
World War I ends	1918	
Civil War ends	1865	
Declaration of Independence signed	1776	
Columbus crosses Atlantic	1492	
Leif Ericson visits North America	1000	

Table B Geologic Events

Event	Number of Years Ago	Reams or Sheets of Paper	Thickness of Paper
End of the last Ice Age	10,000		
Whales evolve	50 million		
Pangaea begins to break up	225 million		
First vertebrates develop	530 million		
Multicellular organisms develop (algae)	1 billion		
First life (bacteria)	3.5 billion		
Oldest known rocks form	4.0 billion		
Age of Earth	4.6 billion		

7. Measure the thickness of a ream of paper. Use this thickness to calculate how thick a stack of paper would need to be to represent how long ago each geologic event occurred. (*Hint:* Use a calculator to multiply the thickness of the ream of paper by the number of reams.) Enter your results in Table B.

Analyze and Conclude

1. Measure the height of your classroom. How many reams of paper would you need to reach the ceiling? How many years would the height of the ceiling represent? Which geologic events listed in Table B would fall on a ream of paper inside your classroom?
2. At this scale, how many classrooms would have to be stacked on top of each other to represent the age of Earth? The time when vertebrates appeared?
3. How many times higher would the thickness of the stack be for the age of Earth than for the breakup of Pangaea?
4. On your model, how could you distinguish one era or period from another? How could you show when particular organisms evolved and when they became extinct?

5. **Think About It** Is the scale of your model practical? What would be the advantages and disadvantages of a model that fit geologic time on a time line 1 meter long?

More to Explore

This model represents geologic time as a straight line. Can you think of other ways of representing geologic time graphically? Using colored pencils, draw your own version of the geologic time scale so that it fits on a single sheet of typing paper. (*Hint:* You could represent geologic time as a wheel, a ribbon, or a spiral.)

SECTION 5 Earth's History

DISCOVER •••ACTIVITY••••

What Do Fossils Reveal About Earth's History?

1. Compare the two fossils in photos A and B. How did these organisms become fossils?

2. Work with one or two other students to study the organisms in the two photos. Think about how these organisms may have lived. Then make sketches showing what each of these organisms may have looked like.

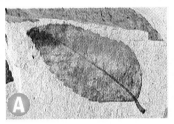

Think It Over

Posing Questions If you were a paleontologist, what questions would you want to ask about these organisms?

GUIDE FOR READING

◆ What were the major events in Earth's geologic history?

◆ What were the major events in the development of life on Earth?

Reading Tip Preview *Exploring Geologic History* on pages 132–135. Make a list of questions you have about Earth's history. Then look for answers as you read.

Your science class is going on a field trip, but this trip is a little out of the ordinary. You're going to travel back billions of years to the earliest days on Earth. Then you will move forward through time to the present. Enter the time machine and strap yourself in. Take a deep breath—you're off!

A dial on the dashboard shows the number of years before the present. You stare at the dial—it reads 4.6 billion years. You peer out the window as the time machine flies above the planet. Earth looks a little strange. Where are the oceans? Where are the continents? How will Earth change over the next billions of years? You'll answer these and other questions about Earth's history as you take this extraordinary trip.

Precambrian Time

Your journey through the first part of Earth's history will need to be very fast. Remember, Precambrian time includes most of Earth's history!

Precambrian Earth **Earth formed from a mass of dust and gas about 4.6 billion years ago.** Gravity pulled this mass together. Over time, Earth's interior became very hot and molten. Hundreds of millions of years passed. Then lava flowed over the surface, building the first continents. An atmosphere formed, and the world was covered with an ocean.

The Earliest Forms of Life Scientists cannot pinpoint when or where life began on Earth. But scientists have found fossils of single-celled organisms in rocks that formed about 3.5 billion years ago. These earliest life forms were probably similar to present-day bacteria. All other forms of life on Earth evolved from these simple organisms.

About 2.5 billion years ago, organisms first began using energy from the sun to make their own food. This process is called photosynthesis. One waste product of photosynthesis is oxygen. As oxygen was released into the air, the amount of oxygen in the atmosphere slowly increased. Over time, organisms evolved that could use oxygen to produce energy from food. These organisms included animals that are like today's sponges and worms. Because they all had soft bodies, these animals left few fossils. However, the evolution of these organisms set the stage for great changes during the Paleozoic Era. You can trace the development of life in *Exploring Geologic History* on pages 132–135.

The Paleozoic Era

Your time machine slows. You watch in fascination as you observe the "explosion" of life that began the Paleozoic Era.

Life Explodes During the Cambrian Period life took a big leap forward. **At the beginning of the Paleozoic Era, a great number of different kinds of organisms evolved.** Paleontologists call this event the Cambrian Explosion because so many new life forms appeared within a relatively short time. For the first time, many organisms had hard parts, including shells and outer skeletons.

At this time, all animals lived in the sea. Invertebrates such as jellyfish, worms, and sponges drifted through the water, crawled along the sandy bottom, or attached themselves to the ocean floors. Recall that invertebrates are animals that lack backbones.

Figure 22 During the early Cambrian period, Earth's oceans were home to many strange organisms unlike any animals that are alive today. The fossil above is an organism of the middle Cambrian called *Burgessia bella* from the Burgess shale.

Brachiopods and trilobites were common in the Cambrian seas. Brachiopods were small ocean animals with two shells. They resembled modern clams. Clams, however, are only distantly related to them.

During the Ordovician (awr duh VISH ee un) and Silurian (sih LOOR ee un) periods, the ancestors of the modern octopus and squid appeared. Some of these organisms, called cephalopods, grew to a length of almost 10 meters. **During this time, jawless fishes evolved. Jawless fishes were the first vertebrates.** A **vertebrate** is an animal with a backbone. These fishes had suckerlike mouths, and they soon became common in the seas.

Life Reaches Land Until the Silurian Period, only one-celled organisms lived on the land. But during the Silurian Period, plants began to grow on land. These first, simple plants grew low to the ground in damp areas. But by the Devonian Period (dih VOH nee un), plants that could grow in drier areas had evolved. Among these plants were the earliest ferns. The first insects also appeared during the Silurian Period.

Figure 23 One of the first amphibians, *Icthyostega* (center), was about 1 meter long. It lived during the late Devonian Period. Another, more fishlike amphibian, *Acanthostega* (bottom), lived at about the same time.

Both invertebrates and vertebrates lived in the Devonian seas. Even though the invertebrates were more numerous, the Devonian Period is often called the Age of Fishes. This is because every main group of fishes was present in the oceans at this time. Most fishes now had jaws, bony skeletons, and scales on their bodies. Sharks appeared in the late Devonian Period.

During the Devonian Period, animals began to invade the land. The first vertebrates to crawl onto land were lungfish with strong, muscular fins. The first amphibians evolved from these fishes. An **amphibian** (am FIB ee un) is an animal that lives part of its life on land and part of its life in water. *Ichthyostega*, shown in Figure 23, was one of the first amphibians.

Throughout the rest of the Paleozoic Era, life expanded over Earth's continents. Other groups of

Figure 24 Forests flourished during the Carboniferous Period. Insects such as dragonflies were common. *Predicting What types of fossils would you expect to find from the Carboniferous Period?*

vertebrates evolved from the amphibians. For example, small reptiles developed during the Carboniferous Period. **Reptiles** have scaly skin and lay eggs with tough, leathery shells. Some types of reptiles became very large during the later Paleozoic.

During the Carboniferous Period, winged insects evolved into many forms, including huge dragonflies and cockroaches. Giant ferns and cone-bearing plants and trees formed vast swampy forests called "coal forests." How did the coal forest get its name? The remains of the coal forest plants formed thick deposits of sediment that changed into coal over millions of years.

Mass Extinction Ends the Paleozoic At the end of the Paleozoic Era, many kinds of organisms died out. This was a **mass extinction,** in which many types of living things became extinct at the same time. **The mass extinction at the end of the Paleozoic affected both plants and animals, on land and in the seas. Scientists do not know what caused the mass extinction, but as much as 95 percent of the life in the oceans disappeared.** For example, trilobites, which had existed since early in the Paleozoic, suddenly became extinct. Many amphibians also became extinct. But not all organisms disappeared. The mass extinction did not affect fishes. Many reptiles also survived.

✓ Checkpoint What were three major events in the development of life during the Paleozoic Era?

Figure 25 *Dimetrodon*, which lived during the Permian Period, was one of the first reptiles. This meat-eater was about 3.5 meters long.

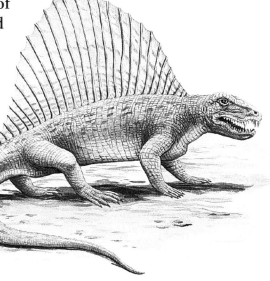

EXPLORING Geologic History

Using the fossil record, paleontologists have created a picture of the different types of common organisms in each geologic period.

PRECAMBRIAN TIME
4.6 billion–544 million years ago

PALEOZOIC ERA
544–245 million years ago

Period	CAMBRIAN	ORDOVICIAN	SILURIAN

544–505 million years ago

505–438 million years ago

438–408 million years ago

Early bacteria

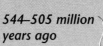
Early algae

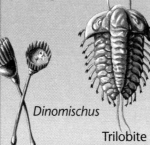
Dinomischus

Trilobite

Sponges

Pikaia

Clam

Jellyfish-like animal

Ediacaran sea pen

Brachiopod

Cephalopod

Jawless fish

Crinoid

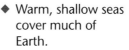

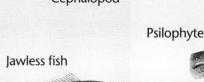
Psilophyte

Eurypterid

Arachnid

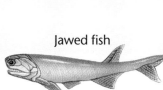
Jawed fish

- Earth forms about 4.6 billion years ago.
- Oceans form and cover Earth about 4 billion years ago.
- Oxygen is present in Earth's atmosphere about 3.5 billion years ago.
- First sedimentary rocks form about 3.5 billion years ago.
- Bacteria appear about 3.5 billion years ago.
- Earth's first ice age occurs about 2.3 billion years ago.
- Soft-bodied, multicellular organisms develop late in the Precambrian.
- First mass extinction probably occurs near the end of the Precambrian.

- Ancient continents include Laurentia and Baltica near the equator and Gondwanaland near the South Pole.
- Shallow seas cover much of the land.
- Great "explosion" of invertebrate life occurs in seas.
- Invertebrates with shells appear, including trilobites, mollusks, and brachiopods.

- Warm, shallow seas cover much of Earth.
- Ice cap covers what is now North Africa.
- Invertebrates dominate the oceans.
- Early vertebrates— jawless fish— become common.

- Early continents Laurentia and Baltica collide.
- Coral reefs develop.
- Fish with jaws develop.
- Land plants appear.
- Insects and spiders appear.

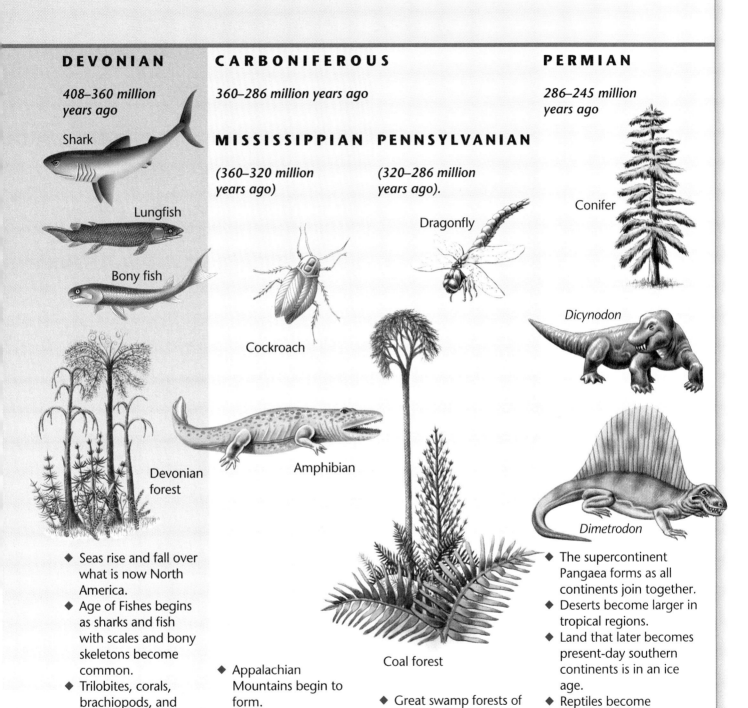

DEVONIAN

408–360 million years ago

Shark

Lungfish

Bony fish

Devonian forest

- Seas rise and fall over what is now North America.
- Age of Fishes begins as sharks and fish with scales and bony skeletons become common.
- Trilobites, corals, brachiopods, and other invertebrates flourish in the oceans.
- Lungfish develop.
- First amphibians reach land.
- Forests grow in swampy areas.

CARBONIFEROUS

360–286 million years ago

MISSISSIPPIAN

(360–320 million years ago)

Cockroach

Amphibian

- Appalachian Mountains begin to form.
- North America and Northern Europe lie in warm, tropical region.
- Cold conditions are present in what is now South America and Africa.

PENNSYLVANIAN

(320–286 million years ago).

Dragonfly

Coal forest

- Great swamp forests of huge, woody trees cover eastern North America and parts of Europe.
- First true reptiles appear.
- Insects become abundant.
- Winged insects appear.

PERMIAN

286–245 million years ago

Conifer

Dicynodon

Dimetrodon

- The supercontinent Pangaea forms as all continents join together.
- Deserts become larger in tropical regions.
- Land that later becomes present-day southern continents is in an ice age.
- Reptiles become dominant on land.
- Warm-blooded reptiles appear.
- Mass extinction causes many marine invertebrates, including trilobites, to disappear.

MESOZOIC ERA
245–65 million years ago

Period TRIASSIC

245–208 million years ago

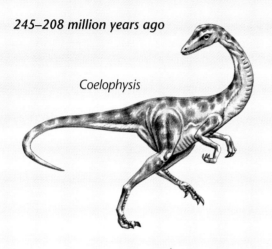

Coelophysis

Morganucodon

Cycad

JURASSIC

208–144 million years ago

Stegosaurus

Megazostrodon

Archaeopteryx

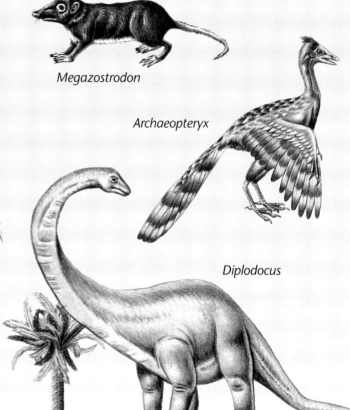

Diplodocus

- Pangaea holds together for much of the Triassic.
- Hot, dry conditions dominate center of Pangaea.
- Age of Reptiles begins.
- First dinosaurs appear.
- First mammals, which evolve from warm-blooded reptiles, appear.
- First turtles and crocodiles appear.
- Conifers, palmlike trees, and ginkgo trees dominate forests.

- Pangaea continues to break apart as North America separates from Africa and South America.
- Sea levels rise in many parts of the world.
- Largest dinosaurs thrive, including *Stegosaurus, Diplodocus,* and *Apatosaurus.*
- First birds appear.
- First flying reptiles, pterosaurs, appear.

CENOZOIC ERA
65 million years ago to the present

CRETACEOUS
144–65 million years ago

Magnolia

Tyrannosaurus rex

Creodonts

Triceratops

◆ Continents move toward their present-day positions, as South America splits from Africa.
◆ Widespread volcanic activity occurs.
◆ First flowering plants appear.
◆ Dinosaurs dominate, including *Tyrannosaurus rex.*
◆ First snakes appear.
◆ Mass extinction at end causes disappearance of many land and marine life forms, including dinosaurs.

TERTIARY
65–1.6 million years ago

Uintatherium

Hyracotherium

Plesiadapis

◆ The Rocky Mountains, Alps, Andes, and Himalayas form.
◆ Continents move into present-day positions.
◆ Continental glacier covers Antarctica about 25 million years ago.
◆ Flowering plants thrive.
◆ First grasses appear.
◆ Age of Mammals begins.
◆ Modern groups such as horses, elephants, bears, rodents, and primates appear.
◆ Mammals return to the seas in the forms of whales and dolphins.
◆ Ancestors of humans evolve.
◆ Continental glaciers repeatedly cover part of North America beginning about 2.5 million years ago.

QUATERNARY
1.6 million years ago to the present

Saber-toothed cat

Megatherium

Homo sapiens

◆ Thick glaciers advance and retreat over much of North America and Europe, parts of South America and Asia, and all of Antarctica.
◆ The Great Lakes form.
◆ Giant mammals flourish in parts of North America and Eurasia not covered by ice. But they become extinct when the Ice Age ends about 10,000 years ago.
◆ Mammals, flowering plants, and insects dominate land.
◆ Modern humans evolve in Africa about 100,000 years ago.

260 million years ago

Figure 26 The supercontinent Pangaea began to break apart about 225 million years ago. *Observing How have North America and South America moved in relation to Africa and Europe?*

Present

Life and Times

1. Place these events in their relative order: continental glaciers retreat; first fish appear; oldest fossils form; human ancestors appear; "explosion" of invertebrates occurs; dinosaurs become extinct; Pangaea forms.

2. Draw a time line and graph these dates:
   - 3.5 billion years ago
   - 544 million years ago
   - 400 million years ago
   - 260 million years ago
   - 65 million years ago
   - 3.5 million years ago
   - 10,000 years ago
   Choose a scale so the oldest date fits on the paper.

Interpreting Data Match each event with the correct date on your time line. How does the time since the dinosaurs became extinct compare with the time since the oldest fossil formed?

The Supercontinent Pangaea

Scientists aren't sure what caused the mass extinction at the end of the Paleozoic. One theory is that Earth's climate changed. But what caused this climate change? Scientists hypothesize that it may have been caused by the slow movement of the continents.

During the Permian period, about 260 million years ago, Earth's continents moved together to form a great landmass, or supercontinent, called Pangaea (pan JEE uh). The formation of Pangaea caused deserts to expand in the tropics. At the same time, sheets of ice covered land closer to the South Pole. Many organisms could not survive the new climate. After Pangaea formed, it broke apart again. Figure 26 shows how the continents moved toward their present-day positions. They moved very slowly—only a few centimeters per year.

The movement of continents is sometimes called continental drift. But the continents don't really "drift." The continents move slowly over Earth's surface because of forces inside Earth.

✓ *Checkpoint* What was Pangaea?

The Mesozoic Era

Millions of years flash by. Your time machine cruises above Pangaea and the landmasses that formed when it broke apart. Watch out—there's a dinosaur! You're observing an era that you've read about in books and seen in movies.

The Triassic Period Some living things survived the Permian mass extinction. These organisms became the main forms of life early in the Triassic Period (try AS ik). Plants and animals that survived included fish, insects, reptiles, and cone-bearing plants called conifers. **Reptiles were so successful during the Mesozoic Era that this time is often called the Age of Reptiles.**

About 225 million years ago, the first dinosaurs appeared. One of the earliest dinosaurs, *Coelophysis,* was a meat eater that had light, hollow bones and ran swiftly on its hind legs. It was about 2.5 meters long.

Mammals also first appeared during the Triassic Period. A **mammal** is a warm-blooded vertebrate that feeds its young milk. Mammals probably evolved from warm-blooded reptiles. The mammals of the Triassic Period were very small, about the size of a mouse or shrew. From these first small mammals, all mammals that live today evolved.

The Jurassic Period During the Jurassic Period (joo RAS ik), dinosaurs became the dominant animal on land. Scientists have identified several hundred different kinds of dinosaurs. Some were plant eaters, while others were meat eaters. Dinosaurs "ruled" Earth for about 150 million years, but different types lived at different times. At 20 meters long, *Dicraeosaurus* was one of the larger dinosaurs of the Jurassic Period. The smallest known dinosaur, *Compsognathus,* was only about 50 centimeters long when fully grown.

Figure 27 *Dicraeosaurus* was a plant-eating dinosaur that lived during the late Jurassic Period.

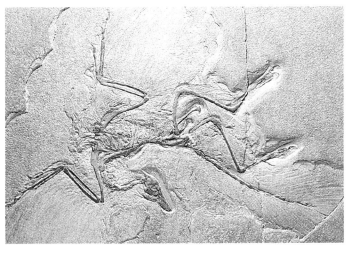

One of the first birds, called *Archaeopteryx*, appeared during the Jurassic Period. The name *Archaeopteryx* means "ancient wing thing." Many paleontologists now think that birds evolved from dinosaurs. During the 1990s, scientists discovered fossils in China with the skulls and teeth of dinosaurs. But these creatures had birdlike bodies and feathers.

Figure 28 From a fossil (above right), paleontologists can tell that *Archaeopteryx* was about 30 centimeters long, had feathers and teeth, and also had claws on its wings. The artist of the illustration (above) has given *Archaeopteryx* colorful feathers.

The Cretaceous Period Reptiles were still the dominant vertebrates throughout the Cretaceous Period (krih TAY shus). Dinosaurs, such as the meat-eating *Tyrannosaurus rex*, ruled the land. But mammals continued to evolve. Flying reptiles and birds competed for places in the sky. The hollow bones and feathers of birds made them better adapted to their environment than the flying reptiles, which became extinct during the Cretaceous Period. In the seas, reptiles such as turtles and crocodiles swam among fishes and marine invertebrates.

The Cretaceous Period also brought new forms of life. Flowering plants evolved. These included leafy trees, shrubs, and small flowering plants like the ones you see today. Unlike the conifers, flowering plants produce seeds that are inside a fruit. The fruit helps the seeds survive.

Another Mass Extinction At the close of the Cretaceous

INTEGRATING SPACE SCIENCE Period, about 65 million years ago, another mass extinction occurred. **Scientists hypothesize that this mass extinction occurred when an object from space struck Earth.** This object was probably an asteroid. Asteroids are rocky masses that orbit the sun between Mars and Jupiter. On rare occasions, the orbits of certain asteroids come dangerously close to Earth. Once in many millions of years, an impact may occur.

When the asteroid hit Earth, the impact threw huge amounts of dust and water vapor into the atmosphere. Many organisms on land and in the oceans died immediately. Dust and heavy clouds blocked sunlight around the world for years. Without sunlight, plants died, and plant-eating animals starved. This mass extinction wiped out over half of all plant and animal groups. No dinosaurs survived. Many other kinds of reptiles also became extinct.

Not all scientists agree that an asteroid impact caused the mass extinction. Some scientists think that climate changes caused by increased volcanic activity were responsible.

Checkpoint *What major groups of organisms developed during the Mesozoic Era?*

The Cenozoic Era

Your voyage through time continues through the Cenozoic Era toward the present. Paleontologists often call the Cenozoic Era the Age of Mammals. During the Mesozoic Era, mammals had a hard time competing with dinosaurs for food and places to live. **The extinction of dinosaurs created an opportunity for mammals. During the Cenozoic Era, mammals evolved adaptations that allowed them to live in many different environments—on land, in water, and even in the air.**

The Tertiary Period During the Tertiary Period, Earth's climates were generally warm and mild. In the oceans, many types of mollusks appeared. Marine mammals such as whales and dolphins evolved. On land, flowering plants, insects, and mammals flourished. When grasses evolved, they provided a food source for grazing mammals. These were the ancestors of today's cattle, deer, sheep, and other grass-eating mammals. Some mammals became very large, as did some birds.

Figure 29 Scientists hypothesize that during the Cretaceous an asteroid hit Earth near the present-day Yucatán Peninsula, in southeastern Mexico.
Relating Cause and Effect How did the asteroid impact affect life on Earth?

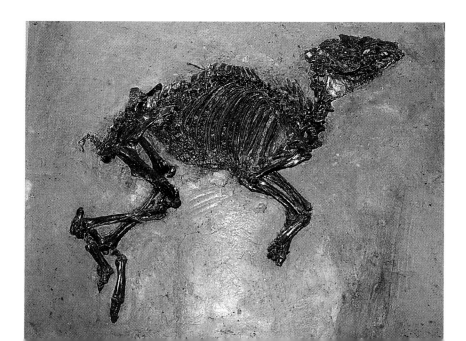

Figure 30 This extinct mammal was related to present-day horses. The fossil formed during the Tertiary Period between 36 and 57 million years ago.

The Quaternary Period The mammals that had evolved during the Tertiary Period eventually faced a changing environment. **Earth's climate cooled, causing a series of ice ages during the Quaternary Period.** Repeatedly, thick continental glaciers advanced and retreated over parts of Europe and North America.

So much of Earth's water was frozen in continental glaciers that the level of the oceans fell by more than 100 meters. Then, about 20,000 years ago, Earth's climate began to warm. Over thousands of years, the continental glaciers melted. This caused sea level to rise again.

In the oceans, algae, coral, mollusks, fish, and mammals thrived. Insects and birds shared the skies. On land, flowering plants and mammals such as bats, cats, dogs, cattle, and humans—just to name a few—became common.

The fossil record suggests that human ancestors appeared about 3.5 million years ago. Modern humans, or *Homo sapiens,* may have evolved as early as 100,000 years ago. By about 12,000 to 15,000 years ago, humans had migrated around the world to every continent except Antarctica.

Your time machine has now arrived back in the present. You and all organisms on Earth are living in the Quaternary Period of the Cenozoic Era. Is this the end of evolution and the changing of Earth's surface? No, these processes will continue as long as Earth exists. But you'll have to take your time machine into the future to see just what happens!

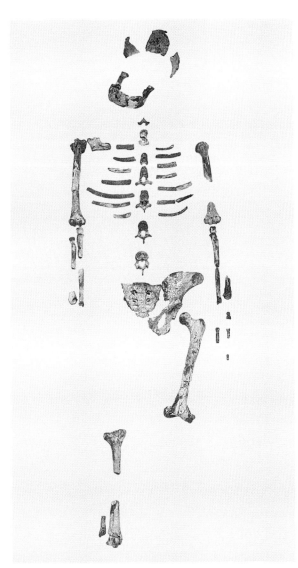

Figure 31 Scientists nicknamed this fossil skeleton Lucy. An early ancestor of modern humans, Lucy lived about 3.3 million years ago.

Section 5 Review

1. What is the "Cambrian explosion"? Why is it important to the history of life on Earth?
2. What was Pangaea? When did it form?
3. How did the extinction of dinosaurs affect the evolution of mammals?
4. What do scientists think was the source of the oxygen in Earth's atmosphere?
5. **Thinking Critically Making Generalizations** How do you think mass extinctions have affected evolution?

Check Your Progress

CHAPTER PROJECT 4

Create illustrations of your portion of the time line. How will you show animals, plants, and environments of that time? When you have finished your illustrations, place them on the time line. Then make a rough draft of your travel brochure. Have a classmate or teacher edit your rough draft before you write the final draft. Do you have all the information about your geologic period that will make a person want to travel there?

SECTION 1 Fossils

Key Ideas

◆ Most fossils form when living things die and are quickly buried by sediment, which eventually hardens and preserves parts of the organisms.
◆ The major kinds of fossils include petrified remains, molds, casts, carbon films, trace fossils, and preserved remains.
◆ The fossil record shows that many different organisms have lived on Earth at different times and that groups of organisms have changed over time.

Key Terms

fossil	mold	scientific
paleontologist	cast	theory
sedimentary rock	carbon film	evolution
petrified fossil	trace fossil	extinct

 SECTION 2 Finding the Relative Age of Rocks

Key Ideas

◆ The law of superposition can be used to determine the relative ages of rock layers.
◆ Scientists also study faults, intrusions, and extrusions to find the relative ages of rock layers.
◆ Index fossils are useful in dating rock layers.

Key Terms

relative age	fault
absolute age	intrusion
law of superposition	extrusion
unconformity	index fossil

 SECTION 3 Radioactive Dating

INTEGRATING CHEMISTRY

Key Ideas

◆ During radioactive decay, the atoms of one element decay into atoms of another element.
◆ Scientists use radioactive dating to determine the absolute ages of rocks.

Key Terms

atom	radioactive decay
element	half-life

 SECTION 4 The Geologic Time Scale

Key Ideas

◆ The basic divisions of the geologic time scale are eras, periods, and epochs.

Key Terms

geologic time scale	invertebrate	epoch
era	period	

 SECTION 5 Earth's History

Key Ideas

◆ A great number of different kinds of living things evolved during the "Cambrian explosion" at the beginning of the Paleozoic Era.
◆ During the Permian Period, the continents joined to form the supercontinent Pangaea.

Key Terms

vertebrate	reptile	mammal
amphibian	mass extinction	

Organizing Information

Concept Map Copy the concept map about fossils onto a piece of paper. Then complete it and add a title. (For more on concept maps, see the Skills Handbook.)

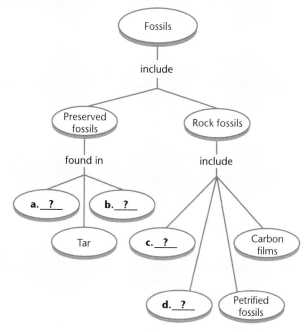

Reviewing Content

For more review of key concepts, see the Interactive Student Tutorial CD-ROM.

Multiple Choice

Choose the answer that best completes each sentence.

1. A hollow area in sediment in the shape of all or part of an organism is called a
   a. mold.   b. cast.
   c. trace fossil. d. carbon film.
2. A gap in the geologic record formed when sedimentary rocks cover an erosion surface is called a(n)
   a. intrusion.
   b. unconformity.
   c. fault.
   d. extrusion.
3. When a radioactive element decays, it releases
   a. atoms.
   b. potassium-40.
   c. particles and energy.
   d. carbon-14.
4. Eras of geologic time are subdivided into
   a. epochs.   b. centuries.
   c. decades.   d. periods.
5. What is an animal that doesn't have a backbone called?
   a. vertebrate   b. mammal
   c. invertebrate d. amphibian

True or False

If the statement is true, write true. If it is false, change the underlined word or words to make the statement true.

6. A dinosaur footprint in rock is an example of a <u>trace fossil</u>.
7. A <u>carbon film</u> is a fossil in which minerals have replaced all or part of an organism.
8. The <u>relative age</u> of something is the exact number of years since an event has occurred.
9. A <u>period</u> is the time required for half of the atoms of a radioactive element to decay.
10. The <u>Paleozoic Era</u> is often called the Age of Reptiles.

Checking Concepts

11. How does a petrified fossil form?
12. Which organism has a better chance of leaving a fossil: a jellyfish or a bony fish? Explain.
13. Describe a process that could cause an unconformity.
14. What evidence would a scientist use to determine the absolute age of a fossil found in a sedimentary rock?
15. What era is often called the Age of Mammals? Why is this appropriate?
16. **Writing to Learn** Imagine that your time machine comes to a halt just as a big event occurs at the end of the Mesozoic Era. Describe what you see, and then describe how this event affects the life you see on Earth.

Thinking Critically

17. **Applying Concepts** Suppose that paleontologists found a certain kind of trilobite in a rock layer at the top of a hill in South America. Then they found the same kind of trilobite in a rock layer at the bottom of a cliff in Africa. What could the paleontologists conclude about the two rock layers?
18. **Making Judgments** If you see a movie in which early humans fight giant dinosaurs, how would you judge the scientific accuracy of that movie? Give reasons for your judgment.
19. **Relating Cause and Effect** When Pangaea formed, the climate changed and the land on Earth became drier. Why do you think that this climate change favored reptiles over amphibians?
20. **Problem Solving** Carbon-14 has a half-life of 5,730 years, while uranium-235 has a half-life of 713 million years. Which would be better to use in dating a fossil from Precambrian time? Explain.

Applying Skills

Use the diagram of rock layers below to answer Questions 21–24.

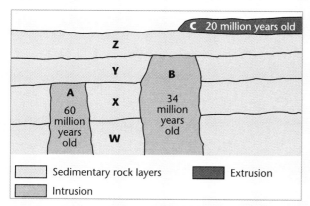

Sedimentary rock layers

Extrusion

Intrusion

21. **Inferring** Which is the oldest layer of sedimentary rock? Which is the youngest? How do you know?

22. **Measuring** What method did a scientist use to determine the age of the intrusion and extrusion?

23. **Interpreting Data** What is the relative age of layer Y (*Hint:* With what absolute ages can you compare it?)

24. **Interpreting Data** What is the relative age of layer Z?

Performance ▼ CHAPTER PROJECT 4 **Assessment**

Project Wrap Up You have completed your illustrations for the time line and travel brochure. Now you are ready to present the story of the geologic time period you researched. Be sure to include the wonderful and awesome things people will see when they travel to this time period. Don't forget to warn them of any dangers that await them.

Reflect and Record In your journal, reflect on what you have learned about Earth's history. What were the most interesting things you found out? If you could travel back in time, how far back would you go?

Test Preparation

Use these questions to prepare for standardized tests.

The diagrams show the index fossils found in rock layers at two different locations. Use the diagrams to answer Questions 25–28.

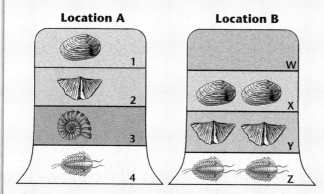

Key

Index fossil	Trilobite	Ammonite	Brachiopod	Clam
Geologic period	Cambrian	Ordovician	Silurian	Devonian

25. According to the law of superposition, the oldest rock layers at Locations A and B are Layers
   a. 2 and Y.   b. 3 and Y.
   c. 4 and Z   d. 1 and W.

26. The youngest rock layer at either location is Layer
   a. 1.   b. X.
   c. 3.   d. W.

27. The index fossil for the Cambrian period is the
   a. ammonite.   b. clam.
   c. trilobite.   d. brachiopod.

28. Layer 1 at Location A and Layer X at Location B both contain fossil clams. These index fossils indicate that both layers formed during the
   a. Devonian Period.
   b. Silurian Period.
   c. Ordovician Period.
   d. Cambrian Period.

The Gift of the Nile

What water—

Lush, fertile lands along the Nile contrast with the scorching desert beyond.

- *flows from south to north?*
- *travels through a scorching desert for much of its length?*
- *nourished a remarkable ancient culture that lasted for 3,000 years?*
- *is the longest river in the world?*

It's the Nile River, which gives life to the Egyptian desert.

More than 5,000 years ago, people first began planting seeds and harvesting crops in the valley of the Nile. The great civilization of Egypt rose in these fertile lands. The Nile supplied water for drinking, growing crops, raising animals, and fishing. When the river flooded every year, it brought a new layer of rich soil to the flood plain.

This productive strip of land was the envy of many nations. Fortunately, the deserts west and east of the Nile River helped protect ancient Egypt from invaders. The river provided a route for trade from central Africa downstream to the Mediterranean Sea. Around 600 B.C., Egypt expanded its trade by digging a canal to the Red Sea.

During the months when the Nile flooded, peasants worked as builders for the Pharaoh, or king. They constructed magnificent pyramids and temples, some of which still stand in the desert today.

Blue water lilies grow in the Nile.

Lifeline of Egypt

The wealth of ancient Egypt and the lives of its people depended on the fertile flood plains that bordered the Nile River. Egyptian society was organized in classes to support agriculture. The Pharaoh was the supreme ruler to whom all Egyptians paid taxes. Below the Pharaoh was a small upper class of priests, scribes, and nobles. Traders and skilled workers, who made tools, pottery, and clothing, formed a small middle class. But the largest group in Egyptian society was the peasants. Peasants used the Nile waters to raise crops that fed all of Egypt.

Priests and nobles recorded the history and literature of ancient Egypt on the walls of monuments and temples. They also wrote on papyrus, a paper made from reeds that grew in marshes along the Nile. Many writings were about the Nile.

When scholars finally found the key to hieroglyphics (hy ur oh GLIF iks), Egyptian writing, they discovered hymns, poems, legends, adventure stories, and lessons for young people. The poem at the right is from a hymn to Hapy, the god of the Nile. "Darkness by day" is the Nile filled with silt.

Egyptian writing, called hieroglyphics, decorates the borders of this poem. ▶

Adoration of Hapy

Hail to you, Hapy,
Sprung from earth,
Come to nourish Egypt!
Of secret ways,
A darkness by day,
To whom his followers sing!
Who floods the fields that Re*
has made,
To nourish all who thirst;
Lets drink the waterless desert,
His dew descending from the sky.

Food provider, bounty maker,
Who creates all that is good!
Lord of awe, sweetly fragrant,
Gracious when he comes.
Who makes herbage for the herds,
Gives sacrifice for every god. . .
He fills the stores,
Makes bulge the barns,
Gives bounty to the poor.

Oh joy when you come!
O joy when you come, O Hapy,
Oh joy when you come!
*Amon-Re, god of the sun

Language Arts Activity

In this poem, Hapy is a personification of the Nile River. When writers and poets use personification, they give an object or animal human qualities. Write your own story or poem using personification. Choose a subject found in nature, such as a mountain, stream, river, or glacier. Jot down human behaviors and actions for your subject—"the stream gurgles, murmurs, and sighs." Before writing, think about the time, place, characters, and sequence of events in your story.

Fertilizing the Fields

In some parts of Egypt, it hasn't rained in years. Only about 3 percent of Egypt can be farmed. The rest is sun-baked desert. But hot weather and the silt and water brought by the Nile River make the Nile Valley highly productive.

The Nile River is the longest river on Earth, stretching 6,650 kilometers. Its drainage basin is about 3.3 million square kilometers. This is larger than that of the Mississippi River. Three major rivers form the Nile—the White Nile, the Blue Nile, and the Atbara.

The source of the White Nile is just south of the equator near Lake Victoria (about 1,135 meters above sea level). A fairly constant volume of water flows north over rapids and through swamp lands to Khartoum. Here the Blue Nile and the White Nile meet to form the great Nile River.

The Blue Nile starts in the eastern plateau of Ethiopia near Lake Tana (about 1,800 meters above sea level). The Atbara River, the last major tributary of the Nile, also flows in from Ethiopia. Between Khartoum and Aswan, the Nile flows north over six cataracts—huge waterfalls. From Aswan to Cairo, the flood plain stretches out on both sides of the river. It gradually widens to about 19 kilometers. Then in Lower Egypt the river branches out to form the Nile Delta.

A view from space shows the Nile River winding through the Sahara Desert. A space probe is at the upper right.

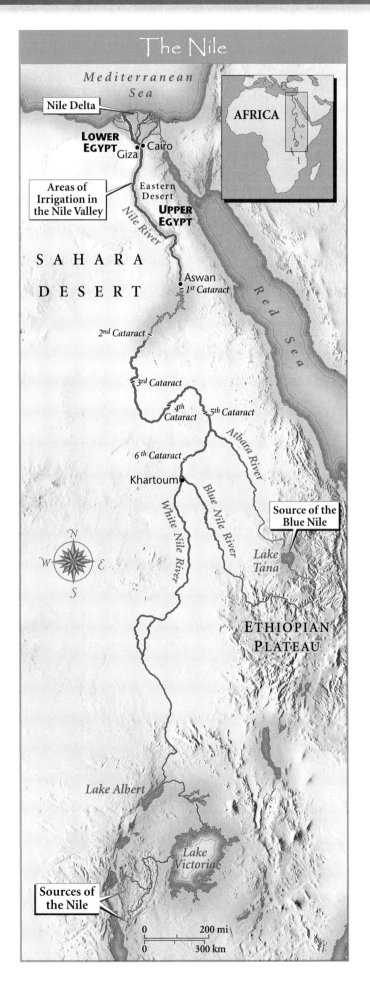

The Nile

Mediterranean Sea

AFRICA

Nile Delta

LOWER EGYPT
Giza • Cairo

Eastern Desert

Areas of Irrigation in the Nile Valley

UPPER EGYPT

Nile River

SAHARA DESERT

Aswan
1st Cataract

Red Sea

2nd Cataract

3rd Cataract

4th Cataract   5th Cataract

Atbara River

6th Cataract

Khartoum

Blue Nile River

Source of the Blue Nile

White Nile River

Lake Tana

ETHIOPIAN PLATEAU

N
W   E
S

Lake Albert

Lake Victoria

Sources of the Nile

0   200 mi
0   300 km

The rushing waters of the Blue Nile carry silt and other sediment from the Ethiopian highlands to the Nile.

Between May and August, heavy rains soak the eastern plateau of Ethiopia and wash rock and silt from the highlands into the Blue Nile. The dark water rushes over rapids and through deep gorges into the Nile River. For thousands of years this rush of water from the Blue Nile and the Atbara caused the seasonal flooding on the Nile. In mid-July, the Nile would begin to rise north of Aswan. When the flood waters went down, the silt remained on the land.

Then in the 1800s and 1900s, Egypt built dams on the Nile to try to control the floodwaters. The Aswan High Dam, the largest of these dams, was completed in 1970. With this dam, the Egyptians finally gained control over annual flooding. The Aswan High Dam holds back water for dry periods and manages surplus water.

In recent years, the population of Egypt and other nations in the Nile basin has grown rapidly. Feeding more people means increasing the area of irrigated cropland. To avoid conflicts, nations must agree to share water. Most of the water in the Blue Nile, for example, comes from Ethiopia.

Yet Egypt and Sudan, the nations farther downstream, use about 90 percent of that water. Today, Ethiopia's growing population needs more Nile water. Using water efficiently and sharing it fairly are essential in the Nile basin.

Science Activities

Use the stream table (pages 86–87) to observe how the Nile builds its delta and how the Aswan Dam affects the river. Pour water into the lower end of the stream table to model the sea.

◆ Make a dam. Cut off the top 2 centimeters from a plastic foam cup. Cut a semicircle for your dam. Cut a small notch in the top of the dam for a spillway.

◆ Start the dripper to create the Nile. Allow it to flow for 5 minutes. What do you observe where the river flows into the sea?

◆ Now place the dam halfway down the river. Scoop out a small, shallow reservoir behind the dam. Observe for 5 minutes.

What effect would you say that the Aswan Dam has on the movement of sediment down the Nile?

Basin Irrigation

The ancient Egyptians may have been the first to irrigate their lands. The slope of the flood plain in Egypt is good for irrigation. From south to north, the land slopes down slightly. The land also slopes slightly down to the desert from the river banks on either side of the Nile.

Egyptians used basin irrigation. They divided the flood plain into a series of basins by building low banks of dirt. When the Nile flooded from July to October, it filled the basins. Then, the water level in the Nile and in the basins gradually dropped. This left a rich sediment layer ready for planting.

In November, peasants plowed the fields and scattered seeds. To push the seeds into the ground, they drove sheep over the fields. Egyptians grew crops of wheat, barley, lentils, onions, beans, garlic, vegetables, and fruits in the Nile Valley. The crops usually could feed all of Egypt. The Egyptians traded any surplus crops for lumber, copper, and beautiful minerals that they used for decorations.

When the fields became dry, peasants brought water from irrigation channels, or deep ditches. They also used a tool called a shaduf to take water directly from the Nile. After the harvest in April, farm animals grazed on the lands until the Nile rose again in mid-July. Then a new cycle began.

The flooding of the Nile determined the lives of early Egyptians. Their year began on the day the Nile began to rise, about July 19 on our calendar. The Egyptians were the first people to have a calendar of 365 days. Their year was divided into 3 seasons based on the Nile's flood cycle. Each season had 4 months of 30 days. At the end of the twelve months, the Egyptians had 5 festival days to complete the year.

The shaduf, still used today, dates back to about 2200 B.C. A wooden beam balances on a pivot, like a plank on a see-saw. Hanging from one end of the beam is a bucket. Balancing at the other end is a large stone. A farmer rocks the beam to scoop water from the Nile. Then the farmer swivels the bucket and empties it into an irrigation channel.

This painting from around 1200 B.C. was found on the wall of the Tomb of Sennedjem in Thebes. The panels show Sennedjem and his wife farming in the afterworld. Sennedjem's wife plants grain. Sennedjem harvests wheat with a sickle (top panel) and plows (middle panel). Egyptians cultivated fruit-bearing trees, such as the date palm (bottom panel).

Social Studies Activities

Divide into groups of three to make a time line of an Egyptian calendar year. Each member of the group should choose a four-month season—flooding, planting, or harvesting—to label and illustrate.

◆ Draw the time line to begin on July 19 and end on July 18.

◆ Divide the time line into 12 months and 5 days.

◆ Label the months and seasons.

◆ Illustrate the seasonal work of the farmers.

The flooded fields of the Nile Delta are separated into lots by irrigation channels.

Measuring the Land

Have you ever measured the length of a room using your feet as the unit of measurement? Around 3000 B.C., ancient Egyptians developed the cubit system of measurement. It was based on the lengths of parts of the arm and hand, rather than the foot. The Egyptian cubit was the length of a forearm from the tip of the elbow to the end of the middle finger. The cubit was subdivided into smaller units of spans, palms, digits, and parts of digits.

Of course, the length of a cubit varied from person to person. So Egypt established a standard cubit, called the Royal Cubit. It was based on the length of the Pharaoh's forearm. The Royal Cubit was a piece of black granite about 52.3 centimeters long. Although the royal architect kept the Royal Cubit, wooden copies were distributed through the land.

Measurement was important to Egyptian life. Every year when the Nile flooded, it wiped out the boundaries for the fields. So after the annual floods, farmers had to measure off new areas. Drawings on the walls of early tombs show that the Egyptians probably had a system for measuring distances and angles on land.

Standard measurement was also necessary for building the massive temples and pyramids that lined the Nile Valley. The cubit stick must have been very accurate, because the lengths of the sides of the Great Pyramid at Giza vary by only a few centimeters.

Egyptians used geometry to measure triangles, squares, and circles to build pyramids. These pyramids at Giza were built around 2500 B.C.

Mathematics Activities

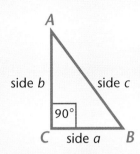

A

side *b*   side *c*

90°

C   side *a*   *B*

To measure fields and build pyramids, the Egyptians needed to understand geometry. They laid out their fields in squares by first making a right triangle. Look at the diagram. The two shorter sides are the legs. The side opposite the right angle is the hypotenuse. The Egyptians might have known that the sum of the squares of the lengths of the legs is equal to the square of the hypotenuse. The equation is $a^2 + b^2 = c^2$. So if side *a* is 3, and side *b* is 4, and side *c* is 5, then $3^2 + 4^2 = 5^2$, or $9 + 16 = 25$.

Now work in groups of 3 to make your own right triangle.

◆ Measure one student's arm to make a cubit stick.

◆ Use the cubit stick to cut one rope 12 cubits long; mark off each of the 12 cubits.

◆ Have 3 students hold the rope at points *A, B,* and *C* so that side *a* is 3 cubits, side *b* is 4 cubits, and *c* is 5 cubits.

Have you made a right triangle? How do you know? How could you make a square?

Tie It Together

Egyptian Exhibition

Plan a brochure to promote a special exhibition on Egypt at a museum. Half the class can focus on ancient Egypt. The other half can find out about the changes that have occurred on the Nile in the last 100 years. Work in small groups to research and assemble the information and illustrations. You might want to include the following:

◆ the Rosetta Stone and hieroglyphics

◆ directions for making a mummy

◆ the Great Pyramid at Giza

◆ history and treasures of King Tutankhamen

◆ religion in ancient Egypt

◆ model of an irrigation system for fields on the Nile

◆ maps of ancient and modern Egypt

◆ construction of the Aswan Dam, 1959–1970

◆ water control on the Nile in Egypt today

◆ Nile Delta today

Think Like a Scientist

Although you may not know it, you think like a scientist every day. Whenever you ask a question and explore possible answers, you use many of the same skills that scientists do. Some of these skills are described on this page.

Observing

When you use one or more of your five senses to gather information about the world, you are **observing.** Hearing a dog bark, counting twelve green seeds, and smelling smoke are all observations. To increase the power of their senses, scientists sometimes use microscopes, telescopes, or other instruments that help them make more detailed observations.

An observation must be an accurate report of what your senses detect. It is important to keep careful records of your observations in science class by writing or drawing in a notebook. The information collected through observations is called evidence, or data.

Inferring

When you interpret an observation, you are **inferring,** or making an inference. For example, if you hear your dog barking, you may infer that someone is at your front door. To make this inference, you combine the evidence—the barking dog—and your experience or knowledge—you know that your dog barks when strangers approach—to reach a logical conclusion.

Notice that an inference is not a fact; it is only one of many possible interpretations for an observation. For example, your dog may be barking because it wants to go for a walk. An inference may turn out to be incorrect even if it is based on accurate observations and logical reasoning. The only way to find out if an inference is correct is to investigate further.

Predicting

When you listen to the weather forecast, you hear many predictions about the next day's weather—what the temperature will be, whether it will rain, and how windy it will be. Weather forecasters use observations and knowledge of weather patterns to predict the weather. The skill of **predicting** involves making an inference about a future event based on current evidence or past experience.

Because a prediction is an inference, it may prove to be false. In science class, you can test some of your predictions by doing experiments. For example, suppose you predict that larger paper airplanes can fly farther than smaller airplanes. How could you test your prediction?

ACTIVITY Use the photograph to answer the questions below.

Observing Look closely at the photograph. List at least three observations.

Inferring Use your observations to make an inference about what has happened. What experience or knowledge did you use to make the inference?

Predicting Predict what will happen next. On what evidence or experience do you base your prediction?

Classifying

Could you imagine searching for a book in the library if the books were shelved in no particular order? Your trip to the library would be an all-day event! Luckily, librarians group together books on similar topics or by the same author. Grouping together items that are alike in some way is called **classifying.** You can classify items in many ways: by size, by shape, by use, and by other important characteristics.

Like librarians, scientists use the skill of classifying to organize information and objects. When things are sorted into groups, the relationships among them become easier to understand.

Classify the objects in the photograph into two groups based on any characteristic you **ACTIVITY** choose. Then use another characteristic to classify the objects into three groups.

Making Models

This student is using a model to demonstrate what causes day and night on Earth. What do the flashlight and the tennis ball in the model represent? **ACTIVITY**

Have you ever drawn a picture to help someone understand what you were saying? Such a drawing is one type of model. A model is a picture, diagram, computer image, or other representation of a complex object or process. **Making models** helps people understand things that they cannot observe directly.

Scientists often use models to represent things that are either very large or very small, such as the planets in the solar system, or the parts of a cell. Such models are physical models—drawings or three-dimensional structures that look like the real thing. Other models are mental models— mathematical equations or words that describe how something works.

Communicating

Whenever you talk on the phone, write a letter, or listen to your teacher at school, you are communicating. **Communicating** is the process of sharing ideas and information with other people. Communicating effectively requires many skills, including writing, reading, speaking, listening, and making models.

Scientists communicate to share results, information, and opinions. Scientists often communicate about their work in journals, over the telephone, in

letters, and on the Internet. They also attend scientific meetings where they share their ideas with one another in person.

On a sheet of paper, write out clear, detailed directions for tying your shoe. Then exchange directions with a partner. Follow your partner's directions exactly. How successful were you at tying your shoe? How could your partner have communicated more clearly? **ACTIVITY**

Making Measurements

When scientists make observations, it is not sufficient to say that something is "big" or "heavy." Instead, scientists use instruments to measure just how big or heavy an object is. By measuring, scientists can express their observations more precisely and communicate more information about what they observe.

Measuring in SI

The standard system of measurement used by scientists around the world is known as the International System of Units, which is abbreviated as SI (in French, *Système International d'Unités*). SI units are easy to use because they are based on multiples of 10. Each unit is ten times larger than the next smallest unit and one tenth the size of the next largest unit. The table lists the prefixes used to name the most common SI units.

Common SI Prefixes

Prefix	Symbol	Meaning
kilo-	k	1,000
hecto-	h	100
deka-	da	10
deci-	d	0.1 (one tenth)
centi-	c	0.01 (one hundredth)
milli-	m	0.001 (one thousandth)

Length To measure length, or the distance between two points, the unit of measure is the **meter (m).** The distance from the floor to a doorknob is approximately one meter. Long distances, such as the distance between two cities, are measured in kilometers (km). Small lengths are measured in centimeters (cm) or millimeters (mm). Scientists use metric rulers and meter sticks to measure length.

Common Conversions

1 km = 1,000 m
1 m = 100 cm
1 m = 1,000 mm
1 cm = 10 mm

The larger lines on the metric ruler in the picture show centimeter divisions, while the smaller, unnumbered lines show millimeter divisions. How many centimeters long is the shell? How many millimeters long is it?

ACTIVITY

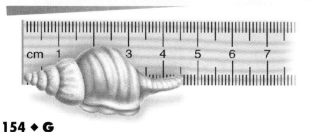

Liquid Volume To measure the volume of a liquid, or the amount of space it takes up, you will use a unit of measure known as the **liter (L).** One liter is the approximate volume of a medium-size carton of milk. Smaller volumes are measured in milliliters (mL). Scientists use graduated cylinders to measure liquid volume.

Common Conversion

1 L = 1,000 mL

The graduated cylinder in the picture is marked in milliliter divisions. Notice that the water in the cylinder has a curved surface. This curved surface is called the *meniscus.* To measure the volume, you must read the level at the lowest point of the meniscus. What is the volume of water in this graduated cylinder?

ACTIVITY

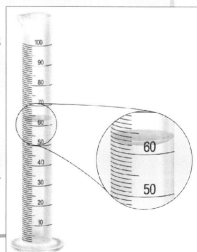

Mass To measure mass, or the amount of matter in an object, you will use a unit of measure known as the **gram** (**g**). One gram is approximately the mass of a paper clip. Larger masses are measured in kilograms (kg). Scientists use a balance to find the mass of an object.

Common Conversion

1 kg = 1,000 g

The mass of the apple in the picture is measured in kilograms.  What is the mass of the apple? Suppose a recipe for applesauce called for one kilogram of apples. About how many apples would you need?

Temperature
To measure the temperature of a substance, you will use the **Celsius scale.** Temperature is measured in degrees Celsius (°C) using a Celsius thermometer. Water freezes at 0°C and boils at 100°C.

ACTIVITY
What is the temperature of the liquid in degrees Celsius?

Converting SI Units

To use the SI system, you must know how to convert between units. Converting from one unit to another involves the skill of **calculating**, or using mathematical operations. Converting between SI units is similar to converting between dollars and dimes because both systems are based on multiples of ten.

Suppose you want to convert a length of 80 centimeters to meters. Follow these steps to convert between units.

1. Begin by writing down the measurement you want to convert—in this example, 80 centimeters.
2. Write a conversion factor that represents the relationship between the two units you are converting. In this example, the relationship is *1 meter = 100 centimeters.* Write this conversion factor as a fraction, making sure to place the units you are converting from (centimeters, in this example) in the denominator.

3. Multiply the measurement you want to convert by the fraction. When you do this, the units in the first measurement will cancel out with the units in the denominator. Your answer will be in the units you are converting to (meters, in this example).

Example

80 centimeters = _____?_____ meters

$$80 \ \text{centimeters} \times \frac{1 \ \text{meter}}{100 \ \text{centimeters}} = \frac{80 \ \text{meters}}{100}$$

$$= 0.8 \ \text{meters}$$

Convert between the following units. **ACTIVITY**
1. 600 millimeters = _?_ meters
2. 0.35 liters = _?_ milliliters
3. 1,050 grams = _?_ kilograms

Conducting a Scientific Investigation

In some ways, scientists are like detectives, piecing together clues to learn about a process or event. One way that scientists gather clues is by carrying out experiments. An experiment tests an idea in a careful, orderly manner. Although experiments do not all follow the same steps in the same order, many follow a pattern similar to the one described here.

Posing Questions

Experiments begin by asking a scientific question. A scientific question is one that can be answered by gathering evidence. For example, the question "Which freezes faster—fresh water or salt water?" is a scientific question because you can carry out an investigation and gather information to answer the question.

Developing a Hypothesis

The next step is to form a hypothesis. A **hypothesis** is a possible explanation for a set of observations or answer to a scientific question. In science, a hypothesis must be something that can be tested. A hypothesis can be worded as an *If...then...* statement. For example, a hypothesis might be *"If I add salt to fresh water, then the water will take longer to freeze."* A hypothesis worded this way serves as a rough outline of the experiment you should perform.

Designing an Experiment

Next you need to plan a way to test your hypothesis. Your plan should be written out as a step-by-step procedure and should describe the observations or measurements you will make.

Two important steps involved in designing an experiment are controlling variables and forming operational definitions.

Controlling Variables In a well-designed experiment, you need to keep all variables the same except for one. A **variable** is any factor that can change in an experiment. The factor that you change is called the **manipulated variable.** In this experiment, the manipulated variable is the amount of salt added to the water. Other factors, such as the amount of water or the starting temperature, are kept constant.

The factor that changes as a result of the manipulated variable is called the responding variable. The **responding variable** is what you measure or observe to obtain your results. In this experiment, the responding variable is how long the water takes to freeze.

An experiment in which all factors except one are kept constant is a **controlled experiment.** Most controlled experiments include a test called the control. In this experiment, Container 3 is the control. Because no salt is added to Container 3, you can compare the results from the other containers to it. Any difference in results must be due to the addition of salt alone.

Forming Operational Definitions
Another important aspect of a well-designed experiment is having clear operational definitions. An **operational definition** is a statement that describes how a particular variable is to be measured or how a term is to be defined. For example, in this experiment, how will you determine if the water has frozen? You might decide to insert a stick in each container at the start of the experiment. Your operational definition of "frozen" would be the time at which the stick can no longer move.

EXPERIMENTAL PROCEDURE

1. Fill 3 containers with 300 milliliters of cold tap water.

2. Add 10 grams of salt to Container 1; stir. Add 20 grams of salt to Container 2; stir. Add no salt to Container 3.

3. Place the 3 containers in a freezer.

4. Check the containers every 15 minutes. Record your observations.

Interpreting Data

The observations and measurements you make in an experiment are called data. At the end of an experiment, you need to analyze the data to look for any patterns or trends. Patterns often become clear if you organize your data in a data table or graph. Then think through what the data reveal. Do they support your hypothesis? Do they point out a flaw in your experiment? Do you need to collect more data?

Drawing Conclusions

A conclusion is a statement that sums up what you have learned from an experiment. When you draw a conclusion, you need to decide whether the data you collected support your hypothesis or not. You may need to repeat an experiment several times before you can draw any conclusions from it. Conclusions often lead you to pose new questions and plan new experiments to answer them.

Is a ball's bounce affected by the height from which it is dropped? Using the steps just described, plan a controlled experiment to investigate this problem.   **ACTIVITY**

Thinking Critically

Has a friend ever asked for your advice about a problem? If so, you may have helped your friend think through the problem in a logical way. Without knowing it, you used critical-thinking skills to help your friend. Critical thinking involves the use of reasoning and logic to solve problems or make decisions. Some critical-thinking skills are described below.

Comparing and Contrasting

When you examine two objects for similarities and differences, you are using the skill of **comparing and contrasting.** Comparing involves identifying similarities, or common characteristics. Contrasting involves identifying differences. Analyzing objects in this way can help you discover details that you might otherwise overlook.

ACTIVITY
Compare and contrast the two animals in the photo. First list all the similarities that you see. Then list all the differences.

Applying Concepts

When you use your knowledge about one situation to make sense of a similar situation, you are using the skill of **applying concepts.** Being able to transfer your knowledge from one situation to another shows that you truly understand a concept. You may use this skill in answering test questions that present different problems from the ones you've reviewed in class.

ACTIVITY
You have just learned that water takes longer to freeze when other substances are mixed into it. Use this knowledge to explain why people need a substance called antifreeze in their car's radiator in the winter.

Interpreting Illustrations

Diagrams, photographs, and maps are included in textbooks to help clarify what you read. These illustrations show processes, places, and ideas in a visual manner. The skill called **interpreting illustrations** can help you learn from these visual elements. To understand an illustration, take the time to study the illustration along with all the written information that accompanies it. Captions identify the key concepts shown in the illustration. Labels point out the important parts of a diagram or map, while keys identify the symbols used in a map.

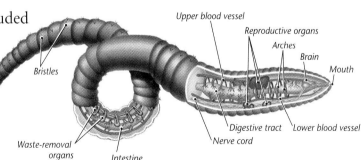

Bristles
Upper blood vessel
Reproductive organs
Arches
Brain
Mouth
Digestive tract
Lower blood vessel
Nerve cord
Waste-removal organs
Intestine

▲ **Internal anatomy of an earthworm**

ACTIVITY
Study the diagram above. Then write a short paragraph explaining what you have learned.

Relating Cause and Effect

If one event causes another event to occur, the two events are said to have a cause-and-effect relationship. When you determine that such a relationship exists between two events, you use a skill called **relating cause and effect.** For example, if you notice an itchy, red bump on your skin, you might infer that a mosquito bit you. The mosquito bite is the cause, and the bump is the effect.

It is important to note that two events do not necessarily have a cause-and-effect relationship just because they occur together. Scientists carry out experiments or use past experience to determine whether a cause-and-effect relationship exists.

ACTIVITY

You are on a camping trip and your flashlight has stopped working. List some possible causes for the flashlight malfunction. How could you determine which cause-and-effect relationship has left you in the dark?

Making Generalizations

When you draw a conclusion about an entire group based on information about only some of the group's members, you are using a skill called **making generalizations.** For a generalization to be valid, the sample you choose must be large enough and representative of the entire group. You might, for example, put this skill to work at a farm stand if you see a sign that says, "Sample some grapes before you buy." If you sample a few sweet grapes, you may conclude that all the grapes are sweet—and purchase a large bunch.

ACTIVITY

A team of scientists needs to determine whether the water in a large reservoir is safe to drink. How could they use the skill of making generalizations to help them? What should they do?

Making Judgments

When you evaluate something to decide whether it is good or bad, or right or wrong, you are using a skill called **making judgments.** For example, you make judgments when you decide to eat healthful foods or to pick up litter in a park. Before you make a judgment, you need to think through the pros and cons of a situation, and identify the values or standards that you hold.

ACTIVITY

Should children and teens be required to wear helmets when bicycling? Explain why you feel the way you do.

Problem Solving

When you use critical-thinking skills to resolve an issue or decide on a course of action, you are using a skill called **problem solving.** Some problems, such as how to convert a fraction into a decimal, are straightforward. Other problems, such as figuring out why your computer has stopped working, are complex. Some complex problems can be solved using the trial and error method—try out one solution first, and if that doesn't work, try another. Other useful problem-solving strategies include making models and brainstorming possible solutions with a partner.

Organizing Information

As you read this textbook, how can you make sense of all the information it contains? Some useful tools to help you organize information are shown on this page. These tools are called *graphic organizers* because they give you a visual picture of a topic, showing at a glance how key concepts are related.

Concept Maps

Concept maps are useful tools for organizing information on broad topics. A concept map begins with a general concept and shows how it can be broken down into more specific concepts. In that way, relationships between concepts become easier to understand.

A concept map is constructed by placing concept words (usually nouns) in ovals and connecting them with linking words. Often, the most general concept word is placed at the top, and the words become more specific as you move downward. Often the linking words, which are written on a line extending between two ovals, describe the relationship between the two concepts they connect. If you follow any string of concepts and linking words down the map, it should read like a sentence.

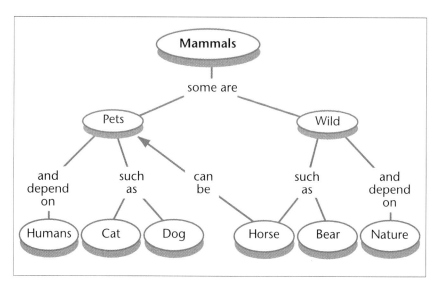

Some concept maps include linking words that connect a concept on one branch of the map to a concept on another branch. These linking words, called cross-linkages, show more complex interrelationships among concepts.

Compare/Contrast Tables

Compare/contrast tables are useful tools for sorting out the similarities and differences between two or more items. A table provides an organized framework in which to compare items based on specific characteristics that you identify.

To create a compare/contrast table, list the items to be compared across the top of a table. Then list the characteristics that will form the basis of your comparison in the left-hand column. Complete the table by filling in information about each characteristic, first for one item and then for the other.

Characteristic	Baseball	Basketball
Number of Players	9	5
Playing Field	Baseball diamond	Basketball court
Equipment	Bat, baseball, mitts	Basket, basketball

Venn Diagrams

Another way to show similarities and differences between items is with a Venn diagram. A Venn diagram consists of two or more circles that partially overlap. Each circle represents a particular concept or idea. Common characteristics, or similarities, are written within the area of overlap between the two circles. Unique characteristics, or differences, are written in the parts of the circles outside the area of overlap.

To create a Venn diagram, draw two over-lapping circles. Label the circles with the names of the items being compared. Write the

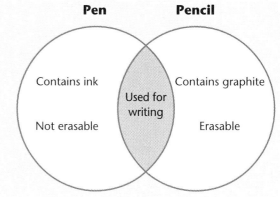

Pen **Pencil**

Contains ink

Used for writing

Contains graphite

Not erasable

Erasable

unique characteristics in each circle outside the area of overlap. Then write the shared characteristics within the area of overlap.

Flowcharts

A flowchart can help you understand the order in which certain events have occurred or should occur. Flowcharts are useful for outlining the stages in a process or the steps in a procedure.

To make a flowchart, write a brief description of each event in a box. Place the first event at the top of the page, followed by the second event, the third event, and so on. Then draw an arrow to connect each event to the one that occurs next.

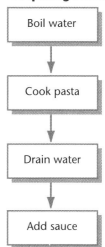

Preparing Pasta

Boil water

↓

Cook pasta

↓

Drain water

↓

Add sauce

Cycle Diagrams

A cycle diagram can be used to show a sequence of events that is continuous, or cyclical. A continuous sequence does not have an end because, when the final event is over, the first event begins again. Like a flowchart, a cycle diagram can help you understand the order of events.

To create a cycle diagram, write a brief description of each event in a box. Place one event at the top of the page in the center. Then, moving in a clockwise direction around an imaginary circle, write each event in its proper sequence. Draw arrows that connect each event to the one that occurs next, forming a continuous circle.

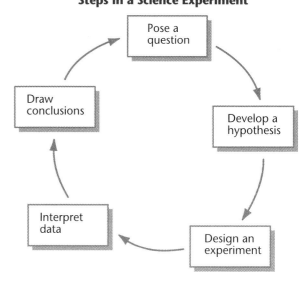

Steps in a Science Experiment

Pose a question

Develop a hypothesis

Design an experiment

Interpret data

Draw conclusions

Creating Data Tables and Graphs

How can you make sense of the data in a science experiment? The first step is to organize the data to help you understand them. Data tables and graphs are helpful tools for organizing data.

Data Tables

You have gathered your materials and set up your experiment. But before you start, you need to plan a way to record what happens during the experiment. By creating a data table, you can record your observations and measurements in an orderly way.

Suppose, for example, that a scientist conducted an experiment to find out how many Calories people of different body masses burn while doing various activities. The data table shows the results.

Notice in this data table that the manipulated variable (body mass) is the heading of one column. The responding variable (for Experiment 1, the number of Calories burned while bicycling) is the heading of the next column. Additional columns were added for related experiments.

CALORIES BURNED IN 30 MINUTES OF ACTIVITY			
Body Mass	Experiment 1 Bicycling	Experiment 2 Playing Basketball	Experiment 3 Watching Television
30 kg	60 Calories	120 Calories	21 Calories
40 kg	77 Calories	164 Calories	27 Calories
50 kg	95 Calories	206 Calories	33 Calories
60 kg	114 Calories	248 Calories	38 Calories

Bar Graphs

To compare how many Calories a person burns doing various activities, you could create a bar graph. A bar graph is used to display data in a number of separate, or distinct, categories. In this example, bicycling, playing basketball, and watching television are three separate categories.

To create a bar graph, follow these steps.

1. On graph paper, draw a horizontal, or *x*-, axis and a vertical, or *y*-, axis.
2. Write the names of the categories to be graphed along the horizontal axis. Include an overall label for the axis as well.
3. Label the vertical axis with the name of the responding variable. Include units of measurement. Then create a scale along the axis by marking off equally spaced numbers that cover the range of the data collected.
4. For each category, draw a solid bar using the scale on the vertical axis to determine the

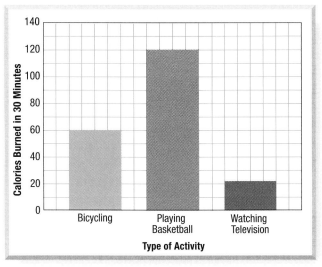

Calories Burned by a 30-kilogram Person in Various Activities

appropriate height. For example, for bicycling, draw the bar as high as the 60 mark on the vertical axis. Make all the bars the same width and leave equal spaces between them.
5. Add a title that describes the graph.

Line Graphs

To see whether a relationship exists between body mass and the number of Calories burned while bicycling, you could create a line graph. A line graph is used to display data that show how one variable (the responding variable) changes in response to another variable (the manipulated variable). You can use a line graph when your manipulated variable is *continuous*, that is, when there are other points between the ones that you tested. In this example, body mass is a continuous variable because there are other body masses between 30 and 40 kilograms (for example, 31 kilograms). Time is another example of a continuous variable.

Line graphs are powerful tools because they allow you to estimate values for conditions that you did not test in the experiment. For example, you can use the line graph to estimate that a 35-kilogram person would burn 68 Calories while bicycling.

To create a line graph, follow these steps.

1. On graph paper, draw a horizontal, or *x*-, axis and a vertical, or *y*-, axis.
2. Label the horizontal axis with the name of the manipulated variable. Label the vertical axis with the name of the responding variable. Include units of measurement.
3. Create a scale on each axis by marking off equally spaced numbers that cover the range of the data collected.
4. Plot a point on the graph for each piece of data. In the line graph above, the dotted lines show how to plot the first data point (30 kilograms and 60 Calories). Draw an imaginary vertical line extending up from the horizontal axis at the 30-kilogram mark. Then draw an imaginary horizontal line extending across from the vertical axis at the 60-Calorie mark. Plot the point where the two lines intersect.

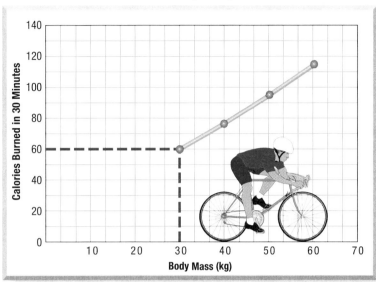

Effect of Body Mass on Calories Burned While Bicycling

5. Connect the plotted points with a solid line. (In some cases, it may be more appropriate to draw a line that shows the general trend of the plotted points. In those cases, some of the points may fall above or below the line. Also, not all graphs are linear. It may be more appropriate to draw a curve to connect the points.)
6. Add a title that identifies the variables or relationship in the graph.

Create line graphs to display the data from Experiment 2 and Experiment 3 in the data table. **ACTIVITY**

You read in the newspaper that a total of 4 centimeters of rain fell in your area in June, 2.5 centimeters fell in July, and 1.5 centimeters fell in August. What type of graph would you use to display these data? Use graph paper to create the graph. **ACTIVITY**

Circle Graphs

Like bar graphs, circle graphs can be used to display data in a number of separate categories. Unlike bar graphs, however, circle graphs can only be used when you have data for *all* the categories that make up a given topic. A circle graph is sometimes called a pie chart because it resembles a pie cut into slices. The pie represents the entire topic, while the slices represent the individual categories. The size of a slice indicates what percentage of the whole a particular category makes up.

The data table below shows the results of a survey in which 24 teenagers were asked to identify their favorite sport. The data were then used to create the circle graph at the right.

Sports That Teens Prefer

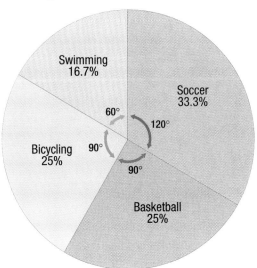

FAVORITE SPORTS

Sport	Number of Students
Soccer	8
Basketball	6
Bicycling	6
Swimming	4

To create a circle graph, follow these steps.

1. Use a compass to draw a circle. Mark the center of the circle with a point. Then draw a line from the center point to the top of the circle.

2. Determine the size of each "slice" by setting up a proportion where x equals the number of degrees in a slice. (NOTE: A circle contains 360 degrees.) For example, to find the number of degrees in the "soccer" slice, set up the following proportion:

$$\frac{\text{students who prefer soccer}}{\text{total number of students}} = \frac{x}{\text{total number of degrees in a circle}}$$

$$\frac{8}{24} = \frac{x}{360}$$

Cross-multiply and solve for x.

$$24x = 8 \times 360$$
$$x = 120$$

The "soccer" slice should contain 120 degrees.

3. Use a protractor to measure the angle of the first slice, using the line you drew to the top of the circle as the 0° line. Draw a line from the center of the circle to the edge for the angle you measured.

4. Continue around the circle by measuring the size of each slice with the protractor. Start measuring from the edge of the previous slice so the wedges do not overlap. When you are done, the entire circle should be filled in.

5. Determine the percentage of the whole circle that each slice represents. To do this, divide the number of degrees in a slice by the total number of degrees in a circle (360), and multiply by 100%. For the "soccer" slice, you can find the percentage as follows:

$$\frac{120}{360} \times 100\% = 33.3\%$$

6. Use a different color to shade in each slice. Label each slice with the name of the category and with the percentage of the whole it represents.

7. Add a title to the circle graph.

ACTIVITY

In a class of 28 students, 12 students take the bus to school, 10 students walk, and 6 students ride their bicycles. Create a circle graph to display these data.

Laboratory Safety

Safety Symbols

These symbols alert you to possible dangers in the laboratory and remind you to work carefully.

Safety Goggles Always wear safety goggles to protect your eyes in any activity involving chemicals, flames or heating, or the possibility of broken glassware.

Lab Apron Wear a laboratory apron to protect your skin and clothing from damage.

Breakage You are working with materials that may be breakable, such as glass containers, glass tubing, thermometers, or funnels. Handle breakable materials with care. Do not touch broken glassware.

Heat-resistant Gloves Use an oven mitt or other hand protection when handling hot materials. Hot plates, hot glassware, or hot water can cause burns. Do not touch hot objects with your bare hands.

Heating Use a clamp or tongs to pick up hot glassware. Do not touch hot objects with your bare hands.

Sharp Object Pointed-tip scissors, scalpels, knives, needles, pins, or tacks are sharp. They can cut or puncture your skin. Always direct a sharp edge or point away from yourself and others. Use sharp instruments only as instructed.

Electric Shock Avoid the possibility of electric shock. Never use electrical equipment around water, or when the equipment is wet or your hands are wet. Be sure cords are untangled and cannot trip anyone. Disconnect the equipment when it is not in use.

Corrosive Chemical You are working with an acid or another corrosive chemical. Avoid getting it on your skin or clothing, or in your eyes. Do not inhale the vapors. Wash your hands when you are finished with the activity.

Poison Do not let any poisonous chemical come in contact with your skin, and do not inhale its vapors. Wash your hands when you are finished with the activity.

Physical Safety When an experiment involves physical activity, take precautions to avoid injuring yourself or others. Follow instructions from your teacher. Alert your teacher if there is any reason you should not participate in the activity.

Animal Safety Treat live animals with care to avoid harming the animals or yourself. Working with animal parts or preserved animals also may require caution. Wash your hands when you are finished with the activity.

Plant Safety Handle plants in the laboratory or during field work only as directed by your teacher. If you are allergic to certain plants, tell your teacher before doing an activity in which those plants are used. Avoid touching harmful plants such as poison ivy, poison oak, or poison sumac, or plants with thorns. Wash your hands when you are finished with the activity.

Flames You may be working with flames from a lab burner, candle, or matches. Tie back loose hair and clothing. Follow instructions from your teacher about lighting and extinguishing flames.

No Flames Flammable materials may be present. Make sure there are no flames, sparks, or other exposed heat sources present.

Fumes When poisonous or unpleasant vapors may be involved, work in a ventilated area. Avoid inhaling vapors directly. Only test an odor when directed to do so by your teacher, and use a wafting motion to direct the vapor toward your nose.

Disposal Chemicals and other laboratory materials used in the activity must be disposed of safely. Follow the instructions from your teacher.

Hand Washing Wash your hands thoroughly when finished with the activity. Use antibacterial soap and warm water. Lather both sides of your hands and between your fingers. Rinse well.

General Safety Awareness You may see this symbol when none of the symbols described earlier appears. In this case, follow the specific instructions provided. You may also see this symbol when you are asked to develop your own procedure in a lab. Have your teacher approve your plan before you go further.

Science Safety Rules

To prepare yourself to work safely in the laboratory, read over the following safety rules. Then read them a second time. Make sure you understand and follow each rule. Ask your teacher to explain any rules you do not understand.

Dress Code

1. To protect yourself from injuring your eyes, wear safety goggles whenever you work with chemicals, burners, glassware, or any substance that might get into your eyes. If you wear contact lenses, notify your teacher.
2. Wear a lab apron or coat whenever you work with corrosive chemicals or substances that can stain.
3. Tie back long hair to keep it away from any chemicals, flames, or equipment.
4. Remove or tie back any article of clothing or jewelry that can hang down and touch chemicals, flames, or equipment. Roll up or secure long sleeves.
5. Never wear open shoes or sandals.

General Precautions

6. Read all directions for an experiment several times before beginning the activity. Carefully follow all written and oral instructions. If you are in doubt about any part of the experiment, ask your teacher for assistance.
7. Never perform activities that are not assigned or authorized by your teacher. Obtain permission before "experimenting" on your own. Never handle any equipment unless you have specific permission.
8. Never perform lab activities without direct supervision.
9. Never eat or drink in the laboratory.
10. Keep work areas clean and tidy at all times. Bring only notebooks and lab manuals or written lab procedures to the work area. All other items, such as purses and backpacks, should be left in a designated area.
11. Do not engage in horseplay.

First Aid

12. Always report all accidents or injuries to your teacher, no matter how minor. Notify your teacher immediately about any fires.
13. Learn what to do in case of specific accidents, such as getting acid in your eyes or on your skin. (Rinse acids from your body with lots of water.)
14. Be aware of the location of the first-aid kit, but do not use it unless instructed by your teacher. In case of injury, your teacher should administer first aid. Your teacher may also send you to the school nurse or call a physician.
15. Know the location of emergency equipment, such as the fire extinguisher and fire blanket, and know how to use it.
16. Know the location of the nearest telephone and whom to contact in an emergency.

Heating and Fire Safety

17. Never use a heat source, such as a candle, burner, or hot plate, without wearing safety goggles.
18. Never heat anything unless instructed to do so. A chemical that is harmless when cool may be dangerous when heated.
19. Keep all combustible materials away from flames. Never use a flame or spark near a combustible chemical.
20. Never reach across a flame.
21. Before using a laboratory burner, make sure you know proper procedures for lighting and adjusting the burner, as demonstrated by your teacher. Do not touch the burner. It may be hot. And never leave a lighted burner unattended!
22. Chemicals can splash or boil out of a heated test tube. When heating a substance in a test tube, make sure that the mouth of the tube is not pointed at you or anyone else.
23. Never heat a liquid in a closed container. The expanding gases produced may blow the container apart.
24. Before picking up a container that has been heated, hold the back of your hand near it. If you can feel heat on the back of your hand, the container is too hot to handle. Use an oven mitt to pick up a container that has been heated.

Using Chemicals Safely

25. Never mix chemicals "for the fun of it." You might produce a dangerous, possibly explosive substance.

26. Never put your face near the mouth of a container that holds chemicals. Many chemicals are poisonous. Never touch, taste, or smell a chemical unless you are instructed by your teacher to do so.

27. Use only those chemicals needed in the activity. Read and double-check labels on supply bottles before removing any chemicals. Take only as much as you need. Keep all containers closed when chemicals are not being used.

28. Dispose of all chemicals as instructed by your teacher. To avoid contamination, never return chemicals to their original containers. Never simply pour chemicals or other substances into the sink or trash containers.

29. Be extra careful when working with acids or bases. Pour all chemicals over the sink or a container, not over your work surface.

30. If you are instructed to test for odors, use a wafting motion to direct the odors to your nose. Do not inhale the fumes directly from the container.

31. When mixing an acid and water, always pour the water into the container first and then add the acid to the water. Never pour water into an acid.

32. Take extreme care not to spill any material in the laboratory. Wash chemical spills and splashes immediately with plenty of water. Immediately begin rinsing with water any acids that get on your skin or clothing, and notify your teacher of any acid spill at the same time.

Using Glassware Safely

33. Never force glass tubing or thermometers into a rubber stopper or rubber tubing. Have your teacher insert the glass tubing or thermometer if required for an activity.

34. If you are using a laboratory burner, use a wire screen to protect glassware from any flame. Never heat glassware that is not thoroughly dry on the outside.

35. Keep in mind that hot glassware looks cool. Never pick up glassware without first checking to see if it is hot. Use an oven mitt. See rule 24.

36. Never use broken or chipped glassware. If glassware breaks, notify your teacher and dispose of the glassware in the proper broken-glassware container. Never handle broken glass with your bare hands.

37. Never eat or drink from lab glassware.

38. Thoroughly clean glassware before putting it away.

Using Sharp Instruments

39. Handle scalpels or other sharp instruments with extreme care. Never cut material toward you; cut away from you.

40. Immediately notify your teacher if you cut your skin when working in the laboratory.

Animal and Plant Safety

41. Never perform experiments that cause pain, discomfort, or harm to animals. This rule applies at home as well as in the classroom.

42. Animals should be handled only if absolutely necessary. Your teacher will instruct you as to how to handle each animal species brought into the classroom.

43. If you know that you are allergic to certain plants, molds, or animals, tell your teacher before doing an activity in which these are used.

44. During field work, protect your skin by wearing long pants, long sleeves, socks, and closed shoes. Know how to recognize the poisonous plants and fungi in your area, as well as plants with thorns, and avoid contact with them. Never eat any part of a plant or fungus.

45. Wash your hands thoroughly after handling animals or a cage containing animals. Wash your hands when you are finished with any activity involving animal parts, plants, or soil.

End-of-Experiment Rules

46. After an experiment has been completed, turn off all burners or hot plates. If you used a gas burner, check that the gas-line valve to the burner is off. Unplug hot plates.

47. Turn off and unplug any other electrical equipment that you used.

48. Clean up your work area and return all equipment to its proper place.

49. Dispose of waste materials as instructed by your teacher.

50. Wash your hands after every experiment.

Physical Map: United States

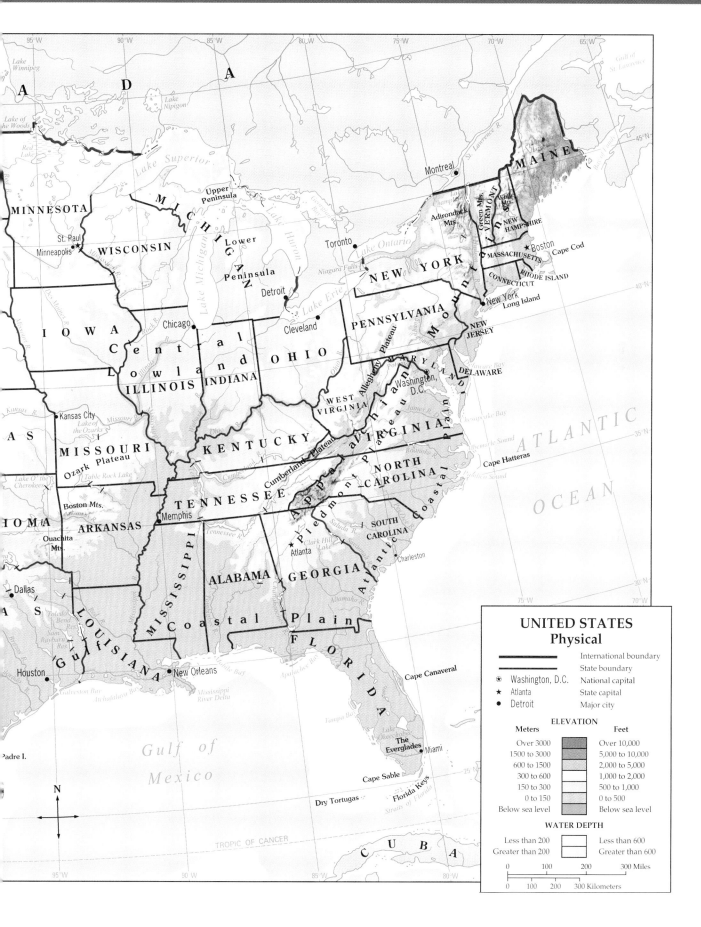

UNITED STATES
Physical

International boundary
State boundary
⊛ Washington, D.C.   National capital
★ Atlanta   State capital
• Detroit   Major city

ELEVATION

Meters		Feet
Over 3000		Over 10,000
1500 to 3000		5,000 to 10,000
600 to 1500		2,000 to 5,000
300 to 600		1,000 to 2,000
150 to 300		500 to 1,000
0 to 150		0 to 500
Below sea level		Below sea level

WATER DEPTH

| Less than 200 | | Less than 600 |
| Greater than 200 | | Greater than 600 |

0   100   200   300 Miles

0   100   200   300 Kilometers

Glossary

abrasion The grinding away of rock by other rock particles carried in water, ice, or wind. (pp. 41, 86)

absolute age The age of a rock given as the number of years since the rock formed. (p. 113)

alluvial fan A wide, sloping deposit of sediment formed where a stream leaves a mountain range. (p. 77)

amphibian A vertebrate that lives part of its life on land and part of its life in water. (p. 130)

atmosphere The mixture of gases that surrounds Earth. The outermost of the four spheres into which scientists divide Earth. (p. 18)

atom The smallest particle of an element. (p. 119)

beach Wave-washed sediment along a coast. (p. 97)

bedrock The solid layer of rock beneath the soil. (p. 49)

biosphere All living things. One of the four spheres into which scientists divide Earth. (p. 18)

carbon film A type of fossil consisting of an extremely thin coating of carbon on rock. (p. 109)

cast A fossil that is a copy of an organism's shape, formed when minerals seep into a mold. (p. 108)

chemical weathering The process that breaks down rock through chemical changes. (p. 43)

conservation plowing Soil conservation method in which the dead stalks from the previous year's crop are left in the ground to hold the soil in place. (p. 60)

continental glacier A glacier that covers much of a continent or large island. (p. 89)

contour interval The difference in elevation from one contour line to the next. (p. 31)

contour line A line on a topographic map that connects points of equal elevation. (p. 31)

contour plowing Plowing fields along the curves of a slope to prevent soil loss. (p. 60)

controlled experiment An experiment in which all factors except one are kept constant. (p. 157)

decomposer Soil organism that breaks down the remains of organisms and digests them. (p. 53)

deflation Wind erosion that removes surface materials. (p. 99)

degree A unit used to measure distances around a circle. One degree equals $\frac{1}{360}$ of a full circle. (p. 22)

delta A landform made of sediment that is deposited where a river flows into an ocean or lake. (p. 77)

deposition Process in which sediment is laid down in new locations. (p. 67)

digitizing Converting information to numbers for use by a computer. (p. 28)

divide The ridge of land that separates one drainage basin from another. (p. 75)

drainage basin The land area from which a river and its tributaries collect their water. (p. 75)

Dust Bowl The area of the Great Plains where wind erosion caused soil loss during the 1930s. (p. 59)

element A type of matter in which all the atoms are the same. (p. 119)

elevation Height above sea level. (p. 15)

energy The ability to do work or cause change. (p. 85)

epochs Subdivisions of the periods of the geologic time scale. (p. 125)

equator An imaginary line that circles Earth halfway between the North and South poles. (p. 21)

era One of the three long units of geologic time between the Precambrian and the present. (p. 124)

erosion The process by which water, ice, wind, or gravity moves weathered rock and soil. (pp. 41, 67)

evolution The process by which all the different kinds of living things have changed over time. (p. 110)

extinct Describes a type of organism that no longer exists anywhere on Earth. (p. 110)

extrusion An igneous rock layer formed when lava flows onto Earth's surface and hardens. (p. 116)

fault A break or crack in Earth's lithosphere along which the rocks move. (p. 115)

flood plain Wide valley through which a river flows. (p. 76)

fossil The preserved remains or traces of living things. (p. 106)

friction The force that opposes the motion of one surface as it moves across another surface. (p. 87)

geologic time scale A record of the geologic events and life forms in Earth's history. (p. 123)

glacier A large mass of moving ice and snow on land. (p. 89)

Global Positioning System A method of finding latitude and longitude using satellites. (p. 33)

globe A sphere that represents Earth's surface. (p. 19)

groundwater Water that fills the cracks and spaces in underground soil and rock layers. (p. 80)

gully A large channel in soil formed by erosion. (p. 73)

half-life The time it takes for half of the atoms of a radioactive element to decay. (p. 120)

hemisphere One half of the sphere that makes up Earth's surface. (p. 21)

humus Dark-colored organic material in soil. (p. 50)

hydrosphere Earth's water and ice. One of the four spheres into which scientists divide Earth. (p. 18)

hypothesis A possible explanation for a set of observations or answer to a scientific question; must be testable. (p. 156)

ice age One time in the past when continental glaciers covered large parts of Earth's surface. (p. 90)

ice wedging Process that splits rock when water seeps into cracks, then freezes and expands. (p. 42)

index fossils Fossils of widely distributed organisms that lived during only one short period. (p. 116)

intrusion An igneous rock layer formed when magma hardens beneath Earth's surface. (p. 116)

invertebrate An animal without a backbone. (p. 124)

karst topography A type of landscape in rainy regions where there is limestone near the surface, characterized by caverns, sinkholes, and valleys. (p. 81)

kettle A small depression that forms when a chunk of ice is left in glacial till. (p. 92)

key A list of the symbols used on a map. (p. 20)

kinetic energy The energy an object has due to its motion. (p. 85)

landform region A large area of land where the topography is similar. (p. 15)

landform A feature of topography formed by the processes that shape Earth's surface. (p. 15)

latitude The distance in degrees north or south of the equator. (p. 22)

law of superposition The geologic principle that states that in horizontal layers of sedimentary rock, each layer is older than the layer above it and younger than the layer below it. (p.114)

lithosphere Earth's solid rock outer layer. One of four spheres into which scientists divide Earth. (p. 18)

litter The loose layer of dead plant leaves and stems on the surface of the soil. (p. 52)

load The amount of sediment that a river or stream carries. (p. 86)

loam Rich, fertile soil that is made up of about equal parts of clay, sand, and silt. (p. 50)

loess A wind-formed deposit made of fine particles of clay and silt. (p.100)

longitude The distance in degrees east or west of the prime meridian. (p. 23)

longshore drift The movement of water and sediment down a beach caused by waves coming in to shore at an angle. (p. 97)

mammal A warm-blooded vertebrate that feeds its young milk. (p. 137)

manipulated variable The one factor that a scientist changes during an experiment. (p. 157)

map projection A framework of lines that helps to show landmasses on a flat surface. (p. 24)

map A model of all or part of Earth's surface as seen from above. (p. 19)

mass extinction When many types of living things become extinct at the same time. (p. 131)

mass movement Any one of several processes by which gravity moves sediment downhill. (p. 67)

meander A looplike bend in the course of a river. (p. 76)

mechanical weathering The type of weathering in which rock is physically broken into smaller pieces. (p. 41)

mold A fossil formed when an organism buried in sediment dissolves, leaving a hollow area. (p. 108)

moraine A ridge formed by the till deposited at the edge of a glacier. (p. 91)

mountain A landform with high elevation and high relief. (p. 16)

mountain range A series of mountains that have the same general shape and structure. (p. 16)

operational definition A statement that describes how to define or measure a particular variable. (p. 157)

oxbow lake A meander cut off from a river. (p. 76)

paleontologist A scientist who studies fossils to learn about organisms that lived long ago. (p. 106)

period One of the units of geologic time into which geologists divide eras. (p. 125)

permeable Characteristic of a material that is full of tiny, connected air spaces that water can seep through. (p. 45)

petrified fossil A fossil in which minerals replace all or part of an organism. (p. 107)

pixels The tiny dots in a satellite image. (p. 27)

plain A landform made up of flat or gently rolling land with low relief. (p. 16)

plateau A landform that has high elevation and a more or less level surface. (p. 17)

plucking The process by which a glacier picks up rocks as it flows over the land. (p. 90)

potential energy Energy that is stored and available to be used later. (p. 85)

prime meridian The line that makes a half circle from the North Pole to the South Pole and that passes through Greenwich, England. (p. 22)

radioactive decay The breakdown of a radioactive element, releasing particles and energy. (p. 120)

relative age The age of a rock compared to the ages of rock layers. (p. 113)

relief The difference in elevation between the highest and lowest parts of an area. (p. 15)

reptile A vertebrate with scaly skin that lays eggs with tough, leathery shells. (p. 131)

responding variable The factor that changes as a result of changes to the manipulated variable in an experiment. (p. 157)

rill A tiny groove in soil made by flowing water. (p. 73)

river A large stream. (p. 74)

runoff Water that flows over the ground surface rather than soaking into the ground. (p. 73)

sand dune A deposit of wind-blown sand. (p. 98)

satellite images Pictures of the land surface based on computer data collected from satellites. (p. 26)

scale Used to compare distance on a map or globe to distance on Earth's surface. (p. 19)

scientific theory A well-tested concept that explains a wide range of observations. (p. 110)

sedimentary rock The type of rock that is made of hardened sediment. (p. 107)

sediment Earth materials deposited by erosion. (p. 67)

sod A thick mass of grass roots and soil. (p. 57)

soil conservation The management of soil to prevent its destruction. (p. 60)

soil horizon A layer of soil that differs in color and texture from the layers above or below it. (p. 51)

soil The loose, weathered material on Earth's surface in which plants can grow. (p. 49)

spit A beach formed by longshore drift that projects like a finger out into the water. (p. 97)

stalactite A calcite deposit that hangs from the roof of a cave. (p. 81)

stalagmite A cone-shaped calcite deposit that builds up from the floor of a cave. (p. 81)

stream A channel through which water is continually flowing downhill. (p. 74)

subsoil The layer of soil beneath the topsoil that contains mostly clay and other minerals. (p. 51)

symbols On a map, pictures used by mapmakers to stand for features on Earth's surface. (p. 20)

till The sediments deposited directly by a glacier. (p. 91)

topographic map A map that shows the surface features of an area. (p. 29)

topography The shape of the land determined by elevation, relief, and landforms. (p. 14)

topsoil Mixture of humus, clay, and other minerals that forms the crumbly, topmost layer of soil. (p. 51)

trace fossils A type of fossil that provides evidence of the activities of ancient organisms. (p. 109)

tributary A stream that flows into a larger stream. (p. 74)

turbulence A type of movement of water in which, rather than moving downstream, the water moves every which way. (p. 88)

unconformity A place where an old, eroded rock surface is in contact with a newer rock layer. (p. 115)

valley glacier A long, narrow glacier that forms when snow and ice build up in a mountain valley. (p. 89)

variable Any factor that can change in an experiment. (p. 157)

vertebrate An animal with a backbone. (p. 130)

weathering The chemical and physical processes that break down rock at Earth's surface. (p. 40)

Acknowledgments

Staff Credits

The people who made up the **Science Explorer** team—representing design services, editorial, editorial services, electronic publishing technology, manufacturing & inventory planning, marketing, marketing services, market research, online services & multimedia development, production services, product planning, project office, and publishing processes—are listed below.

Carolyn Belanger, Barbara A. Bertell, Suzanne Biron, Peggy Bliss, Peter W. Brooks, Christopher R. Brown, Greg Cantone, Jonathan Cheney, Todd Christy, Lisa J. Clark, Patrick Finbarr Connolly, Edward Cordero, Robert Craton, Patricia Cully, Patricia M. Dambry, Kathleen J. Dempsey, Judy Elgin, Gayle Connolly Fedele, Frederick Fellows, Barbara Foster, Paula Foye, Loree Franz, Donald P. Gagnon Jr., Paul J. Gagnon, Joel Gendler, Elizabeth Good, Robert M. Graham, Kerri Hoar, Joanne Hudson, Linda D. Johnson, Anne Jones, Toby Klang, Carolyn Langley, Russ Lappa, Carolyn Lock, Cheryl Mahan, Dotti Marshall, Meredith Mascola, Jeanne Y. Maurand, Karen McHugh, Eve Melnechuk, Natania Mlawer, Paul W. Murphy, Cindy A. Noftle, Julia F. Osborne, Judi Pinkham, Caroline M. Power, Robin L. Santel, Suzanne J. Schineller, Emily Soltanoff, Kira Thaler-Marbit, Mark Tricca, Diane Walsh, Pearl Weinstein, Merce Wilczek, Helen Young.

Illustration

Kathleen Dempsey: 17, 25, 34, 46, 56, 82, 118T, 126
John Edwards & Associates: 22, 23T, 31, 44, 86, 87, 91, 95, 107
GeoSystems Global Corporation: 15, 23B, 24, 55, 58, 59, 75T, 77, 90, 98
Andrea Golden: 8T, 11B, 151
Martucci Design: 30, 50
Morgan Cain & Associates: 33, 50, 52–53, 66, 68, 69, 75B, 88, 99, 120, 122, 123, 124
Matt Myerchak: 35, 61, 141, 143
Ortelius Design Inc.: 20, 21, 136
Matthew Pippin: 51, 78–79, 92–93
Walter Stuart: 11T, 8–9
J/B Woolsey Associates: 37, 42, 63, 73, 111, 114, 117, 118B, 132–135

Photography

Photo Research Paula Wehde
Cover Image David Muench Photography

Nature of Science
Page 8, University of Wyoming Public Relations; **10 both**, Courtesy of Kelli Trujillo; **11**, University of Wyoming Public Relations.

Chapter 1
Pages 12–13, Tom Bean; **14**, The Granger Collection, NY; **16t**, Tom Bean; **16b**, David Muench Photography; **18**, ESA/PLI/The Stock Market; **19 both**, Russ Lappa; **20t**, Bodleian Library, Oxford, U.K.; **20b**, The Granger Collection, NY; **21t, br**, The Granger Collection, NY; **21bl**, British Library, London/Bridgeman Art Library, London/Superstock; **26t**, Russ Lappa; **26b, 27 both**, Earth Satellite Corporation/Science Photo Library/Photo Researchers; **28tl**, Geographix; **28tr**, Bob Daemmrich/Stock Boston; **29t**, Richard Haynes; **29b**, Robert Rathe/Stock Boston; **31**, Paul Rezendes; **32**, U.S. Geological Survey; **33t**, Ken M. Johns/Photo Researchers; **34**, Richard Haynes; **37**, U.S. Geological Survey.

Chapter 2
Pages 38–39, Mike Mazzaschi/Stock Boston; **40**, Russ Lappa; **41l**, Ron Watts/Westlight; **41r**, Jerry D. Greer; **42l**, Breck P. Kent/Animals Animals/Earth Scenes; **42r**, Susan Rayfield/Photo Researchers; **43l**, John Sohlden/Visuals Unlimited; **43m**, E.R. Degginger/Photo Researchers; **43r**, Gerald & Buff Corsi/Visuals Unlimited; **45t**, Chromosohm/Sohm/Photo Researchers; **45b**, Breck P. Kent/Animals Animals/Earth Scenes; **47**, Richard Haynes; **48**, John G. Ross/Photo Researchers; **49t**, Richard Haynes; **49b**, Rod Planck/TSI; **54**, J. M. Labat/Jacana/Photo Researchers; **56**, Richard T. Nowitz/Photo Researchers; **57t**, Richard Haynes; **57b**, Jim Brandenburg/Minden Pictures; **58**, Corbis; **59**, AP/Wide World Photos; **60t**, Larry Lefever/Grant Heilman Photography; **60b**, Jim Strawser/Grant Heilman Photography; **61**, John G. Ross/Photo Researchers.

Chapter 3
Pages 64–65 & 66, Jim Steinberg/Photo Researchers; **67**, Paul Sequeira/Photo Researchers; **68t**, Eric Vandeville/Gamma-Liaison Network; **68b**, Thomas G. Rampton/Grant Heilman Photography; **69**,Steven Holt; **70–71**, Richard Haynes; **72**, Photo Disc; **72–73**, Walter Bibikow/The Viesti Collection; **73t**, Runk Schoenberger/ Grant Heilman Photography; **74**, Inga Spence/Tom Stack & Associates; **75**, David Ball/The Stock Market; **76l**, Glenn M. Oliver/Visuals Unlimited; **76r**, Index Stock Photography, Inc.; **77t**, E.R. Degginger; **77b**, NASA/SADO/Tom Stack & Associates; **80**, Chuck O'Rear/Westlight; **81**, *St. Petersburg Times*/Gamma-Liaison; **82**, Russ Lappa; **83**, Richard Haynes; **84**, Doug McKay/TSI; **85t**, Richard Haynes; **85b**, Eliot Cohen; **89t**, Richard Haynes; **89b**, Mark Kelley/Stock Boston; **91**, Grant Heilman Photography; **94**, Craig Tuttle/The Stock Market; **96**, Randy Wells/TSI; **97**, E.R.I.M./TSI; **98t**, Richard Haynes; **98b**, Jess Stock/TSI; **99**, Breck P. Kent; **100**, Connie Toops; **101**, Craig Tuttle/The Stock Market.

Chapter 4
Pages 104–105, Phil Degginger; **106t**, John Cancalosi/Stock Boston; **106b**, Flowers & Newman/Photo Researchers; **107**, Francois Gohier/Photo Researchers; **108 both**, Runk/Schoenberger/Grant Heilman Photography; **109t**, Breck P. Kent; **109b**, Tom Bean; **110**, Howard Grey/TSI; **111tl**, Khalid Ghani/Animals Animals; **111tr**, Frans Lanting/Minden Pictures; **111mr**, The Natural History Museum, London; **111bl**, John Sibbick; **112**, Sinclair Stammers/Science Photo Library/Photo Researchers; **113**, Richard Haynes; **114**, Jeff Greenberg/Photo Researchers; **116l**, G.R. Roberts/Photo Researchers; **116r**, Tom Bean; **116b**, Breck P. Kent; **119**, Mitsuaki Iwago/Minden Pictures; **121**, James King-Holmes/Science Photo Library/Photo Researchers; **125t**, Fletcher & Baylis/Photo Researchers; **125 inset**, John Cancalosi/Tom Stack & Associates; **127**, Richard Haynes; **128l**, Breck P. Kent; **128r**, Runk/Schoenberger/ Grant Heilman Photography; **129r**, The Natural History Museum, London; **129l**, **130**, John Sibbick; **131t**, ©The Field Museum, Neg. # CSGEO 75400c.; **131b**, Natural History Museum/London; **137**, 1989 Mark Hallett; **138l**, Jane Burton/Bruce Coleman; **138r**, David M. Dennis/Tom Stack & Associates; **139t**, D. Van Ravensswaay/Photo Researchers; **139b**, C.M. Dixon; **140**, John Reader/Science Photo Library/Photo Researchers.

Interdisciplinary Exploration
Page 144t, Robert Caputo/Stock Boston; **144–145b**, David Sanger Photography; **145l**, Brian Braker/Photo Researchers; **146**, NASA; **147**, Groenendyk/Photo Researchers; **148–149b**, Thomas J. Abercrombie/National Geographic Society; **148 inset**, Robert Caputo/Stock Boston; **149t**, Robert Caputo/Stock Boston; **150**, David Ball/The Picture Cube; **151**, Richard Haynes.

Skills Handbook
Page 152, Mike Moreland/Photo Network; **153t**, Foodpix; **153m**, Richard Haynes; **153b**, Russ Lappa; **156**, Richard Haynes; **158**, Ron Kimball; **159**, Renee Lynn/Photo Researchers.